THE BAMBOO SHOOT

THE BAMBOO SHOOT

THE STORY OF THE 2ND AIRBOAT PLATOON

AS TOLD IN

THE MEMOIRS OF A DRAFTEE'S SOJOURN IN VIETNAM
1967-1968

JAMES PARKER WOLLNER

To order additional copies of this book, contact:
Xlibris Corporation
1-888-795-4274
www.Xlibris.com
Orders@Xlibris.com
24108

CONTENTS

POEMS . . . MAYBE

WHERE ARE THEY NOW?

FINDING LOST BROTHERS

This book is dedicated to,

HARRY FRANKLIN CARVER

He will forever rest in the hands of God.

*If you light a candle in a very dark place,
it shines a long way.*

Thomas A. Dooley MD. USN

FOREWORD

The phone call was unexpected and posed a real challenge: match the caller's name to an image after thirty-five years. As I struggled with the puzzle, he uttered the key word: "airboats". With the speed of a system password opening protected files, a whole era of my history, long dormant, reopened and leapt for the connections in what he was saying. As he mentioned names, nicknames, shared experiences, meetings, other phone conversations, his efforts to locate members of the airboat unit, and the spouse of a fallen comrade, memories surfaced in blinding flashes. It was as though I were rewinding a video tape, searching in reverse for the caller's point in time.

The caller that day was Jim Wollner, author of the memoir you are about to enjoy. Before locating me that day, Jim had made an exhaustive effort to reconstruct our airboat unit and in the ensuing months, through sheer tenacity and resolve, he reunited our disassociated souls for a reunion. The idea of getting together again seemed implausible at first, since we were settled in different parts of the country and few had made contact in all those years. Jim pulled the plans together though and as he did, they developed a cascading impetus of their own, culminating in an emotional and exceedingly satisfying assembly at the Vietnam Veterans Memorial in Washington, DC. Jim also organized a moving tribute to a member of the unit whose name is indelibly etched in that solemn gray granite. During our few days together, thanks to Jim's efforts and persistence, we were able to rekindle relationships which, forged in combat, require little nurturance and are diminished only by our own demise.

Beyond the gift of bringing us together again, Jim has now done us the immeasurable favor of recording in this book some of the essence of the airboat unit. It is the story of a randomly selected, disparate group of new arrivals to Vietnam, who learned only later that they had "volunteered" to initiate the Army's airboat program. The idea was to exploit the unique characteristics of the Everglades-type swamp buggy in the wetlands, waterways and flooded rice paddies of South Vietnam. The first military mission assigned these green, young recruits was to design, develop, test and implement the armed waterborne combat platforms. It was an objective that challenged every one of us, often to our limits, but it also afforded many uncommon but not necessarily unpleasant memories. In this labor of love, Jim introduces in colorful anecdotes the airboats and the young soldiers who molded them into a proficient, uniquely suited tactical unit. (My personal favorite is an episode we shared securing the "Transphibian Tree-crusher.") Admirably, he captures the effects of an unconventional war on a group of ordinary Americans without seeking a depressive catharsis.

For those of us who were a part of the effort, it was an experience unique in our lifetime: tempering yet rewarding. We are in Jim Wollner's debt not only for immortalizing our efforts and the sacrifices of those who are no longer with us, but also for giving us again the camaraderie we shared so long ago . . .

Norman E. Stone Jr.
LTC (Ret.) AUS
(Former 2nd Airboat Platoon Leader)

PROLOGUE

It was February 6, 1967, and it was my 21st birthday. I remember thinking that now I can legally go to bars and not have any cares about being arrested for underage drinking. My mother had made my favorite dinner of pot roast as well as a birthday cake, but I couldn't wait to go out to a bar and order a drink!

Three months earlier, I had left my job at Schering Corporation to go to college full time; unfortunately I flunked out and got a job driving a truck for a distributor of scientific apparatus and chemicals to schools and pharmaceutical companies.

As I was cutting the cake, Mom handed me a letter from my local draft board. Talk about "bad timing", I was ordered to report at 8:00 AM on April 13, 1967, for induction into the armed forces of the United States. I guess my days of carefree living were about to end, before they got started . . .

On the date ordered I reported to the local draft board in Montclair. After the initial check in me and about 30 others boarded a bus for the Induction center in Newark. We arrived in Newark and were herded into the Induction Center. All of us were given a thorough examination, both physical and mental. After we finished with the exams we were told to form several lines and then told to count off by fours. There were a hundred of us so it took a few minutes, I was number three. When we finished all number fours were told to step forward. They did and were now going to be Marines so line up and move to the bus outside, they were going to Parris Island, SC. The rest of us were given the oath after which we were told to take one step forward. With that step we were now members of the US Army. We got on another waiting bus and were driven to Ft. Dix, NJ, where we would go through basic training. I was some what happy on hearing this because if nothing else, I was still in NJ, close to home. Unfortunately Ft. Dix had no room since it was currently filled with National Guard troops. After spending most of the day there, we were ordered onto the buses. Once seated, we were informed that we were taking a scenic trip to Fayetteville, NC and Ft Bragg. The problem with this was it 7:00 pm. At Fort Bragg we would spend the next eight weeks of hell. This was the home of the 82nd airborne and all the drill sergeants were "gung ho" for airborne. For me who at 21 and out of shape this really sucked. Eight weeks later I had a whole new attitude, as well as a new body 40 lbs. lighter.

I had expected to have a leave after basic, but instead boarded another bus. We were going to Ft. Jackson, SC, for advanced infantry training. The Army determined that my MOS was 11C10 or heavy weapons infantry. Translated this was to learn how to shoot mortars. A more disturbing factor was that Ft. Jackson was a Vietnam training facility, meaning that the majority of the graduates were bound for Vietnam. This really sucked, too! During the latter part of our training, the Newark riots broke out and our unit was put on alert. There was some racial tension in our unit, but the bottom line was that you had to rely on your buddy regardless of what color the guy was, so "don't sweat the small shit"! Eight weeks later when we finished training, we got our assignments and as luck would have it, I was Vietnam bound. It never really dawned on me that I would go since I was an only child and my mother was severely crippled. This coupled with the fact that my father was already retired, would exempt me from going. Boy! Was I wrong! While on leave I wrote to my Congressman, Peter Rodino, to see if he could get my orders changed. I was placed on a congressional hold while my case was looked at. After my leave was up I was to report to McGuire AFB to await the outcome. Two days later it came; I was leaving courtesy of the Air Force that afternoon. We flew from McGuire to Elmendorf in Alaska to Tokota in Japan and finally to "beautiful" Ton Son Nhut in Saigon, Vietnam.

THE STORY

OF

THE 2ND AIRBOAT

PLATOON

1967-1968

DATE: 9/26/1967
TIME: 1200 HRS
LOCATION: TON SON NHUT AIRBASE, SAIGON,
REPUBLIC OF VIETNAM

"I GOTTA GET OUT OF THIS PLACE IF IT'S THE . . . ."

September 26, 1967, an auspicious day. I arrived at Ton Son Nhut airport in Saigon, the Republic of Viet Nam. According to my orders, I was slated to go to the First Air Cavalry Division.

Upon exiting the aircraft, the heat and humidity was unbelievably oppressive. It hit like a slap in the face and added to the scared and forlorn feeling I already had. If ever a person felt so totally alone, it was me.

All personnel on the plane were ordered to get on the buses parked nearby. As soon as we were on them, we were informed of our destination. It was early afternoon, but I could see very little. There were heavy screens covering the windows, which inhibited our ability to see clearly. I found out later that these screens prevented the Viet Cong or their sympathizers from tossing grenades through the windows. We were concerned about moving off the airbase because the driver and one guard had weapons. They told us that we were on our way to the 90th replacement Battalion at Long Binh, just outside of Saigon.

DATE: 9/26/67
TIME: 1300 HRS.
LOCATION: 90TH REPLACEMENT BN. LONG BINH, SOUTH VIETNAM-NORTHEAST OF SAIGON

"WHERE HAVE ALL THE SOLDIERS GONE?"

We arrived safely and were taken to the mess hall and told that there would be two formations each day. At these formations our names would be called and that of the unit with which we would be spending the next year of our lives. KP and other choice details would be assigned daily. This was the SOP, standard operating procedure, for all FNGs. Two days later on the 28th, my name was called.

It was a bright, sunny morning when me, and the names of three people on the plane with me were called. All four of us were to go to the 9th Infantry Division. None of us had ever heard of the 9th Division before so we were in a quandry. We asked a sergeant walking by and he said, "IT'S RIGHT DOWN THE ROAD". I thought, GREAT! Things were finally looking up. We were near Saigon and we would probably be guarding the capital. At least it would be safer than jumping out of choppers in the boonies with the 1st cavalry.

DATE: 9/28/1967
TIME: 1000 HRS.
LOCATION: CAMP BEARCAT, HOME OF THE 9TH INF.
DIV.—EAST OF SAIGON

"WHAT YOU DON'T KNOW WON'T HURT YOU", RIGHT!

Two hours later we arrived at Camp Bearcat, home of the 9th Infantry Division. Much to my chagrin, I found out that the AO, area of operations, of the 9th was the entire Mekong Delta. The optimism I felt earlier evaporated into the steamy morning mist. I had visions of slogging and crawling through the sucking, oozing, and stinking mud, humping a 4.2 mortar. God, please, there must be someway out of this!

That morning we were issued our uniforms, jungle boots, flak vests and most important, our M-16s. For some reason I felt a little safer now that I could defend myself against the "inscrutable" Asian enemy. As new guys, we were assigned the usual details such as perimeter guard, KP and general policing of the areas, and, most important, taught the fine art of "shit burning". Details will follow later in the story.

In the evening, after a long day of serving in the mess hall, I was very tired, but the croaking frogs and insufferable humidity made it impossible to sleep. After nodding off for a few minutes, I was awakened for guard duty: this was truly "no rest for the weary". I also hadn't showered in three days. The smell of us must have been ripe, but no one seemed to notice. On the way to the trucks, I met another kid from Belleville, but he was on the way to his unit so there was no chance to talk. I also found out that I was scheduled to go to B Company 3rd of the 39th Infantry after a week of in-country training.

Everyone had to undergo this week of training, from the highest to lowest in rank, as it was mandatory before being released to the individual units.

We were given indoctrination lectures regarding the locals and refresher courses in booby traps, local customs, first aid, and drugs like marijuana. There was a class on the "chieu hoi" program. This was a hoot! After a Viet Cong soldier would shoot at you all day and then run out of ammo, he would throw his weapon down, raise his hands and holler "chieu hoi". We must take him a prisoner. He then would be reeducated to help us. I thought this was nonsense. How can the army believe in such fairy tales?

In the final days of this training, we were scheduled to set up a night ambush. This ambush would be set up on the local rubber plantation next door to camp Bearcat.

DATE: 10/5/1967
TIME: 0800 HRS.
LOCATION: RUBBER PLANTATION, OUTSIDE OF
CAMP BEARCAT

WHAT ARE WE FIGHTING FOR? MICHELIN TIRES!

We marched to this rubber plantation, not very far from the base camp, and proceeded to settle in to our positions. All of us were scared shitless. No one had any idea what to expect and our leaders would only say to be constantly on guard. We then were ordered to dig foxholes, so dig we did. It was late in the day; there we were laboring under the gaze of the rubber trees, which seemed to stand at attention. I stared back at these trees as they stood in perfect formation as far as the eye could see. They were, in fact, a beautiful sight to behold, especially in the waning light of the day.

The NCO's in charge told us to make sure our ponchos were kept handy since it would rain at a moment's notice. As dusk turned into night, I became very uneasy and held my weapon closer. The trees all began to move, or so I thought, and eerie shadows appeared to dance in and out of them frightening me even more—so much for their beauty now. The longer the night progressed, the more things we saw: lights, probably flashlights in the distance, movement near the tree lines, a Viet Cong sniper maybe, a column of enemy soldiers, then nothing.

Mosquitoes and spiders were also "bugging us", making life in a foxhole very uncomfortable. Adding to our woes, right on cue, it rained so now we were not only itchy, sweaty, tired, and scared, you can add soggy and wet. Our ponchos were of little help. I can say, with some accuracy, that I am finally not the only one feeling sorry for myself—all of us did!

Mercifully, morning came and I, along with everyone else, breathed a super huge sigh of relief. We had survived our first night in the boonies of Vietnam without any incidents. On our march back to camp, a zillion kids appeared all wanting "chop chop" from "numba one GI". We gave them any food we had left over.

VIGNETTE 1: RUBBER TREES

"I'M LIKE A RUBBERBALL . . . BOUNCY, BOUNCY . . ."

There are many rubber plantations in the Republic of Viet Nam. The French brought the rubber trees to Vietnam when it was under colonial control. Most of these plantations, if not all, were owned by a few wealthy French families.

Upon my arrival in RVN, I was assigned to the 9TH Division located at Camp Bearcat. This camp was adjacent to a very large rubber plantation. The owners hated the Americans because as the camp expanded, more and more land was needed, and this meant more of their trees would be destroyed. I could understand how they felt, but "SIN LOI"—an old Vietnamese saying meaning "sorry about that". The French are arrogant people and did not like us anyway, so fuck them.

The rubber trees are without a doubt one of the most magnificent sights I have ever seen. When I first saw them I was in awe and at night they scared the crap out of me, but still they were beautiful.

In every plantation the trees all looked the same. In the unordered and chaotic world of Vietnam, these trees stand alone in their perfect symmetry. They stood at attention like soldiers in gray uniforms with dark green helmets, in perfect formation. Even the cut scars that dripped the raw latex were all in the same place on the different trees.

I learned after our initial week of in-country training that the lights we saw at night moving through the trees were those of the workers checking on the flow of sap. The initial fear I had was, however, a lesson that I always followed because it is dangerous to trust anyone or anything, especially any movement at night. Someone said that there are only two kinds of people in Vietnam, the quick and the dead. I believe I am here today because I followed this dictum each and every day that I spent in this country.

The rubber trees are a symbol of this quixotic country. They seemed to be an island of tranquility in a sea of death, destruction and chaos. They were almost OZ-like in their ordered calm until you stepped out and into the brutal, bloody world of war.

DATE: 10/6/196
TIME: 0630 HRS.
LOCATION: CAMP BEARCAT, NORTHEAST SAIGON

"OH LORD! WON'T YOU BUY ME
A MERCEDES BENZ . . . ?"

We returned to Camp and ate hot chow in the mess hall. We were given the rest of the day off and I used it to catch up on my letters home. Two things suddenly happened that changed my life and all things considered, especially in hindsight, proved to be for the best.

I was sitting on my cot writing home when all of a sudden I heard some shouting. One of the companies in the MRF, Mobile Riverine Force, the 3rd of the 39th Infantry, the unit to which I was going, had been ambushed and had taken many casualties. New replacements were needed as soon as possible. Needless to say, I was extremely unhappy at the prospect of going there. Less than an hour later the second event happened that was to change my life. There was active solicitation for volunteers for a new unit that was to be formed involving the use of airboats.

Airboats, what the hell were they? No one had ever heard of them or seen them. After thinking about it for a good two seconds, my hand shot up and I volunteered for this unit. They say never volunteer for anything in the Army. To this day I don't know why I raised my hand, but I am damn glad I did.

The interviews for joining this unit were held the next morning. Those of us who did volunteer were told that these boats were extremely dangerous and more than likely we'd come home in a body bag. Isn't that another pleasant thought!

The interview was conducted by a Major from an infantry unit. I figured that I would rather get killed riding in a boat than dying in the mud and slime. I really was determined to get into this unit.

Each of us was interviewed alone. The Major asked me a few mundane questions like, where are you from? What would your parents say if you got killed? (What a stupid question!) Were you married? Did you know how to swim? What was the most dangerous thing you ever did? I pondered this last question a few moments and then blurted out: "I used to drive a dragster that could do the quarter mile in 7 seconds". The Major's eyes lit up and I knew he was impressed. He asked a few more questions about drag racing and seemed to like my responses. Thank God I knew more than he did about the subject of drag racing and was accepted. Accepted into what though? Still gnawing at me was what the heck was an Airboat?

Later that same day we were all assembled but still lacked a leader. A spec 4 was picked and temporarily put in charge; his name was Wade T. Nail and he was from Texas. His tenure was short-lived because an hour later a new E-5 was assigned to us by the name of Harry Carver. He would be our platoon sergeant. There was another E-5 with him named Dennis Caughlin. He had just made E-5 so Carver outranked him.

The Major told us that we would be on TDY, temporary duty, for training with a unit that was very experienced in the use of Airboats. TDY, depending on where you were being sent, meant extra money in your pocket. This money would be used to cover your expenses. We wondered to what country we would be going. Would you believe that again our hopes were dashed? The place is "in country"! It was a Special Forces detachment that had been operating airboats for the past couple of years and they were extremely experienced in their tactical use. Our TDY pay amounted to no more than about four extra dollars a day, WHOOPEE!! I guess it was since beer only cost 10 cents a can! Further information would be given to us on a "need to know" basis. In the meantime get some sleep since we would be leaving very early in the A.M.

DATE: 10/8/1967
TIME: 0600 HRS.
LOCATION: ON THE WAY TO CAO LANH, WEST OF
SAIGON

"THE EARLY BIRD GETS THE WORM"
OR THE GREEN WEENIE!

It was early the next morning and still dark when we boarded the Caribou, an Army transport plane that is designed to land on very short airstrips. The Special Forces unit was based at a place called Cao Lanh. This was up the Mekong River and to the west of Saigon. We would be training with this unconventional unit for approximately 3 to 4 weeks. All we needed to bring were three sets of fatigues, a toothbrush and our weapons. Off we flew to parts unknown; it was now October 8, 1967.

As the sun rose over this country, it gave us a much different perspective than seeing it from the ground. It is covered with rivers, canals, rice paddies, and jungle, broken up by dirt roads and an occasional village or town. This seems a calm and idyllic country, in a setting of greenery and silence, especially a couple of thousand feet in the air. Thirty minutes later we were informed that we would be landing and to buckle up because the landing strip was a short one-, it would be" very interesting". We wondered what that meant! A few minutes passed and then we found out! The landing strip was a large driveway; it seemed about 50 feet . . . maybe! The pilot, however, was unconcerned so why should we worry? Our landing was routine and our stomachs landed a few minutes later!

On the ground to meet us was a Green Beret master sergeant who looked very unhappy. Having to shepherd FNG regular army personnel was not his favorite thing. But shepherd us he did, through the town of Cao Lahn and out to the villa complex at which his unit was based. We would not be domiciled in the villa, but in the barracks across the road. The area where we were to sleep had raised platforms off the ground with rolled up mosquito netting. We were told that this would keep most of the bugs and other crawling things that came out at night from biting us. After stowing our gear we were told to report to the dining room for a welcoming speech by the unit commander.

Major Marachek was the man in charge of the unit. He greeted all of us and laid out the rules that we "WILL" follow during our stay here. His words were stern, but surprisingly fair, and all of us liked what we heard. We would obey all our superiors without question, especially our training NCO, Sergeant Barker, the same person who greeted us. Sgt. Barker was British and had the accent to prove it. He also had a quiet but confident air about him. He was the ideal instructor.

We would eat in the dining room at the villa, but all other times were spent training at our quarters across the road. Since this was the weekend, we would have to help ourselves in the dining room as the staff had off! During the week the dining room staff would serve us. We had trouble believing what we heard, the dining room staff? When Major Marachek finished, we were told to settle in. We later learned that Major Marachek was a veteran of the German army, the Canadian army, and the French Foreign Legion before he joined the Special Forces. This was a tough cookie, not a person to mess with or get him pissed at you. It seemed to me that many of the Special Forces were foreigners—maybe that was good.

The compound in which we were living was across the road from the villa, surrounded by concertina and barbed wire, as well as claymore mines strategically located every few feet and covering all areas of access. The area was bordered on one side by the road and on the other by a canal approximately 60 feet wide. There was a reinforced gate that opened to the canal and enclosed a marina where the airboats were docked. The canal serviced the town of Cao Lanh and the villages along its banks, giving them access to the Mekong River.

Once we settled in, it was time for dinner and we were again escorted to the dining room in the villa. We were told that we would have to cook our own steaks. The only condition was that you eat all you take; this was a standing order and one you eagerly followed. It was a resort hotel here, and more than that, you were treated with a modicum of civility which is rare in the army. Everyone here was a drinker and there was a well stocked bar. We were all allowed to use it when we were off duty. There was even a floating card game; and many of us participated in this. There were also showers and flush toilets; this place was paradise! When it comes time for R&R, here's where I want to come!

DATE: 10/9/1967
TIME: 0800
LOCATION: SPECIAL FORCES CAMP, JUST OUTSIDE
CAO LANH

"MEN WHO MEAN JUST WHAT THEY SAY . . ."

We started our training the next day. We learned some simple procedures about the boats and how they operate. We learned about their armament. They had .30 cal machine guns on them, not the standard M-60 with which we were familiar. We were given a crash course on their care, maintenance, and operation. After lunch we learned how to start and how to dock the boats, all within the small marina of course. Tomorrow we would start our familiarization ride and begin to learn just what the airboats could do.

The next morning we were allowed to take the boats for a spin, although very slowly. So many mistakes were made that we feared that we would never learn how to handle them. As each day progressed, we became better and better, but still we weren't allowed to try them at full throttle. The days passed quickly and as our proficiency increased we were allowed to increase the speed. We stayed close to the marina never venturing more than a klick either up or down the canal. One day Sgt. Barker took us up the canal to a small village. As we passed through the outskirts, a shot rang out and hit the water right next to me. Sitting on the left gas tank was Tommy

Reynolds; Mark Kizzire was on the right. Because of the noise of the engine, it was difficult to hear where the shot came from, but Sgt. Barker's reaction was very swift immediately ordering the boats to shore. After a few minutes of trying to find where the shot came from, he came back very annoyed and questioned all on the boat. Tommy said he heard a muffled shot and saw the bullet land in the water next to us. I saw the same thing and confirmed what Tommy said, convinced that I was the target. I was the first person in our unit to get shot at and it really scared me. To the Special Forces unit this continued to be a big deal because the village was supposed to be pacified and they did not like to have enemy snipers in their backyard.

After another week of training we followed the canal south past Cao Lahn and down to the Mekong River. The canal seemed to open into a large fanlike delta; we were finally allowed to open up. The speed of the boats and the wind in our faces was intoxicating. We couldn't get enough; we instantly all became airboat junkies.

During the off hours we watched movies in the dining room that was set up with chairs. This week it was a western, Stagecoach, starring Ann Margaret; cowboys and Indians, just like us! We also played poker, which for some reason, I never seemed to win. I wonder why?—Sgt. Carver did!

One very important topic that was stressed during our training was booby traps. The enemy had a penchant for making life miserable for airboats and Special Forces, in general. They devised a system of stringing piano wire between poles that held fishing traps. As one drove the airboat this wire could cleanly decapitate or severely injure anyone standing at the machine gun or sitting in the driver seat. We would never see it until the damage was done. To solve this, a large piece of angle iron was welded to the gun mounts. This piece of iron was taller than the man standing by the gun, thus protecting him and the driver from the wire. Another tactic of Charley was to string a trip wire attached to grenades or a claymore. When you pulled on the wire the explosive would go off spraying shrapnel all over the place. This was only effective if we were going slowly, 20 or 25 mph. If you were going fast your speed would take you, hopefully, safely out of the kill zone.

We learned other tactics, too, including how to jump rice paddy dikes. If an airboat is tooling around at 40 mph and hits a dike that is not wet, it stops instantly; if your seat belt is unfastened, you didn't! You have to go straight at the dike, execute a 180 spraying it with water to make it slick, make another 180, and like "shit through a goose" over the dike you go!

After another week of training, our little group became proficient in all aspects of the airboat use, but we had yet to go to an actual combat mission. To be really knowledgeable and to see how we would react in certain situations, this was a must! The night before we were to leave for Don Phouc, Tommy Reynolds told me that he had discharged his weapon and the bullet hitting the water was from his gun. He was afraid to say anything before because he didn't want to get into trouble. I was pissed at him because he had scared the shit out of me at the time but secretly glad it was not the enemy. We never divulged this secret to Sgt. Barker or for that matter, Sgt. Carver either.

The Mike force base we were going to, a place called Don Phouc near the Cambodian border, was located in the Plain of Reeds. This was one of the many bases that the Special Forces had throughout the area. We would take the boats on this journey, and to do this, we had to go about 50 klicks, 35 to 40 of which would be on the Mekong River.

All during this time we were kept in the dark about enemy activity; it seemed that they didn't exist. This was about to change, for sister A-team base was overrun further up river, and there were only two survivors. There were also reports that two battalions of NVA regulars had infiltrated into the area where we were going. Needless to say we all had reservations but were confident that our training would serve us well.

DATE: 10/15/1967
TIME: MORNING
LOCATION: ON MEKONG RIVER GOING TO DON
PHOUC AND THE PLAIN OF REEDS,
SPECIAL FORCES BASE, NORTHWEST
OF CAO LANH

"UP THE CREEK WITHOUT A PADDLE"

The Mekong was as muddy and daunting as a river could be. From eye level, it seemed a mile wide and the fear of it was seared into our souls. We had only seen it from the air and at the end of a canal, but having to drive the airboats on it was a much different story. It was an awesome and humbling experience. Its vast expanse was breathtaking. Actual ships traveled on this river delivering their goods all the way to Phnom Penh, the capitol of Cambodia; it was mind-boggling. Driving the airboats was like paddling a rowboat in the ocean—without oars!

Sgt. Barker had us stay very close to the shore or else we would be swamped, as the water was extremely rough and the wakes of passing freighters created even more waves. Airboats are able to go 40 mph, but plying this river, we were lucky to make 20. It took us nearly three hours when finally we turned into a canal that led into the Plain of Reeds.

Before we realized it, there we were and its magnificence was beyond comprehension. It was absolutely stunning! As far as the eye could see, solid greens broken only by hillocks rising out of the water but still surrounded by green. When I say green, I don't mean it all looked the same color, but greens of so many different hues it was unbelievable. I was struck dumb by the beauty of this land and wondered how it could change and become so brutal and deadly in a heartbeat. As we continued our journey, we came upon a group of fisherman checking their fish traps. Sergeant Barker signaled to us to keep going, as we would arrive at our destination shortly. I found out later that the fishermen we saw were probably not fishermen at all but most likely NVA infiltrators. As we were never involved in a hostile action, the First Sergeant thought, "discretion was the better part of valor", so we just kept going. Upon arrival at the reinforced A-team compound of Don Phuoc we settled in and immediately cleaned our boats, getting them ready for action.

Our first assignment was to patrol the area between our base and the Cambodian border 2 klicks away. A nung, more about them later, was assigned to each of our boats. There were no roads or signposts, only water and reeds. The villages we came across were mostly built on stilts above the water. Women, children, and old people populated these villages. The men and boys were probably out fishing with their fellow Viet Cong or NVA regulars. We would go out in two groups of four boats, each group going in different directions in a circle, eventually meeting, and then continuing on and ending where we started. Because this area was so large and our boats were able go anywhere, vast areas were patrolled regularly. We saw nothing, not even the fishermen that were there the day before.

We learned, sometimes the hard way, to keep our mouths shut unless one wanted to see how grasshoppers or other bugs taste! There is so much animal and insect life in these reeds, even in the midst of war.

One day in the late afternoon an unseen enemy opened fire on us. No one was hit, but we returned fire and tried to outflank the area where we thought the gunfire was coming. We were prevented from doing so because a Cambodian checkpoint was too close and watching the action were Cambodian border guards. We were not allowed to cross the border under any circumstances. If we did this, we would create an international incident. The VC and NVA could shoot at us with impunity while flipping us the bird at the same time. They knew we could not pursue them, at least not today. What we learned later was that the Special Forces would exact revenge, of that there was no doubt.

This Special Forces unit was unique in that only a handful of their soldiers were American. The Mike force at Don Phuoc had only four Americans, excluding us; the rest of the soldiers were "Nungs". These soldiers were descendants of Chinese and Cambodian mercenaries, left over and on the losing side of various Chinese invasions. They were fiercely loyal to the Special Forces, as both the VC as well as the South Vietnamese Army held them in disdain. When the VC ran across one of their villages, they would rape their women and steal any food. If they found any children, they would use them as pack animals. Needless to say, this was the main reason for the Nung's loyalty, this and cash. Between the SF and the Nungs we learned that there is no gentlemanly way to fight a war. No quarter was given to either side, and when we did go into Cambodia, we sure didn't stop to get our passports stamped. This occurred of course, only when no one was looking. The border itself was so ill defined that no one could be held responsible for any mistaken border crossings. The VC knew they had the luxury of the Cambodian border in which to hide. This was true only if there was a checkpoint or border patrol nearby. Most of their staging areas were deep inside Cambodia and the NVA operated here with impunity.

Our stay at Don Phouc was by no means a happy one. The SF personnel in charge thought it would be funny to let us to eat only indigenous rations, or IR's as they were known, during our stay with them. These rations were repugnant to the eye, nose, and taste buds, but the Nungs loved them. They consisted of dried rice and fish or shrimp, to which they added water, preferably hot. The fishy and rotten smell was overpowering. We were all starving by the second day because none of us would eat this disgusting food. During one of our missions a baby heron managed to get in my boat. The Nungs took it; they said for a pet, but later it was in their stew pot, along with the IRs. This was supposed to entice us to eat now that, as this delicacy was added.

The next day was the 17th of October, and we happened upon a small village just a few klicks away from the border; it could have even been in Cambodia. We were lucky enough to find an open-air stall that sold canned goods and fresh fruit. We bought oranges and bananas. The canned goods were limited to sardines; how old were they? Only King Oscar knew. There was canned pineapple which we knew not because of the printing but because of the picture on it. The writing on the cans was in Chinese; they were a product of Red China. We bought all we could, for if nothing else we could at least live on these items until we returned to Cao Lanh. We prayed that it would be sooner rather than later. We all longed for its dining room and a nice steak dinner. After a few more days of hunger, our prayers were answered and we returned back down the river to Cao Lanh with smiles on our faces because in a few hours we would finally be dining in luxury. Alas! It was only for one meal. Our training period had ended and we soon had to go back to Bearcat. All of us wanted to stay and work with the

Special Forces because the officers and enlisted men talked to each other as equals. Let us also not over look the quality of the food, too. It took us a few hours to pack. The villa and life here would be just another Vietnam memory.

The second group of volunteers would be coming soon and we had to make room for them. A new chapter was now waiting be written in the story of Airboats in Viet Nam and the future Second Airboat Platoon.

VIGNETTE 2:
CAO LANH AND THE NUNGS

A SICILIAN BLOOD FEUD . . . ASIAN STYLE!

The town of Cao Lahn is a fairly large one. It is the province capital, located on a major canal about two klicks from the Mekong River. On the town's outskirts was a villa housing the Special Forces unit to which we were assigned for training. We lived across the road from the villa in a long barrack—type building in a heavily fortified compound, bordered on one side by the road and on the other side the canal. There were guard towers in this compound not only to protect all within but also monitor the canal traffic. Across the canal from us was a small village populated by the Nung soldiers.

The Nungs, as stated earlier, love Americans and hate the Vietnamese and the Viet Cong. They are excellent warriors and their ability to fight a war is without question. These were the indigenous people, who fought assimilation into Vietnamese society and who worked with the various Special Forces A-Teams throughout this part of Vietnam.

The local Vietnamese seemed to get along well with the Nungs, mostly because of trade. They sold them produce and fruits on a daily basis. Most of the trade was done via sampans which they rowed right up to the village or compound gate. We even bought bananas and oranges and other fruits and vegetables from them; the oranges had a dark green skin but were very sweet.

The location of the compound was a great place to train. The canal was wide enough so we could avoid making mistakes of hitting anything. After a week or two of learning the fundamentals, we ventured down the canal to the entrance of the Mekong.

The area surrounding the camp lulled us all into a false sense of security. Even though there was no enemy activity, a few klicks away a similar SF camp was overrun by the VC so we were all on edge. During the day there was much traffic on the canal but nighttime was very different—nothing moved. It made us very nervous. Later on we came to love the darkness and welcomed the envelope of the night.

After a few more days training we would be off for parts unknown to a place in the plain of reeds called Don Phouc.

VIGNETTE 3: BOOBY TRAPS

"FOOLS RUSH IN WHERE WISE MEN FEAR TO TREAD"

The Viet Cong were masters at setting booby traps. This form of warfare caused the American soldier more grief than anything else in the war. More casualties were incurred by this means than actual face-to-face combat with the enemy.

Booby traps are designed to inflict severe damage on the person who trips them. It is mainly a weapon of terror and made to inflict grievous and devastating injuries, including the loss of limbs and groin injuries, and then is designed to instill psychological damage in others coming to the victim's aid; and they do.

The gooks would use anything they could find for this weapon: c-ration cans packed full of explosives, nails, and wire which when detonated, sent pieces of shrapnel into any personnel nearby. One would quickly learn what NOT to throw away.

The enemy also used sharpened bamboo stakes smeared with human excrement, called punji stakes. This device caused not only injury from the puncture but also massive infection. They were strategically placed in holes or on the side of trails so when you dove for cover, you would be impaled.

They loved to set traps in tunnels. They especially liked to use scorpions, spiders and krait snakes. Crawling through the tunnel, baskets of critters would be strategically placed along the route. When you hit a trip wire, they would be released and fall onto your back. If they were kraits and you got bitten, you didn't have a chance; they were called two-steppers, because after being bitten you would walk two steps and die! Thank heaven I was a rather large person, only men of small stature could go into these tunnels.

Another favorite item that the VC loved to get their hands on was unexploded ordnance. The Cong attached their own detonators to it, and, voila! a very effective booby trap. Another favorite of theirs was a type that when stepped on, you heard a "POP", and it would spring up about waist high, and then explode. If you did not immediately drop and hug the ground, you were dead or severely injured. In most cases your reaction was not fast enough, thus you got a ticket home, sans limbs or guts or in a box. Our first platoon leader, Lieutenant Hoskins, who left our group to join the First platoon, was later killed trying to disarm one that he found. He should have stayed with our platoon. Hoskins was another West Point grad whose name now appears on the "WALL" and on West Point's Honor Roll.

Another favorite of the "Cong" was to stretch piano wire across canals and/or set trip wires across trails. This would be attached to claymores and would explode as you pulled the wire. These were also a very effective anti personnel device.

Booby traps, if nothing else in this country, justified my volunteering for airboats. Riding is far superior to walking and better for your health!

DATE: 10/22/1967
TIME: 1000 HRS
LOCATION: CAMP BEARCAT, EAST OF SAIGON

"HURRY UP AND WAIT AND WAIT"

Today we found out that our boats would not arrive from the States for another month. We also found out that we had been assigned a lieutenant and that our unit was officially designated as the 2nd Airboat Plt. The group that followed us was the 1st Airboat Plt, even though it was not the first trained. If one asks why, the only answer is "it's the army way".

This gave us a chance to get the lay of the land at Bearcat and to see what it offered. The camp was continually growing, and more and more luxuries were becoming available. The PX had ice cream and hamburgers at the snack bar. These were a semblance of normality, set in an abnormal place. We also were assigned the usual details that needed to be done. We became experts in the art of KP and other necessary duties as well.

Someone in authority had an idea that we should be kept on water so as not to lose any knowledge we had gained. There was a company that was using Boston whalers, based out of a place called Tan Tru. This was the 2nd of the 60th infantry, part of the Riverine Force, which used whalers for transporting troops across canals and rivers. Wouldn't it be great for us to go there! For the next couple of days we just lounged around, read or caught up on letters home till D-day. On October 26th we left Bearcat, via Chinook, for a base called Tan Tru.

DATE: 10/26/67
TIME: LATE MORNING
LOCATION: TAN TRU, SOUTH OF SAIGON

"I'M GOING TO GET A TRUE TAN OR TAN TRU"

Upon our arrival we were disappointed that there was nowhere to "hang our hats". It didn't help matters that we were here only temporarily and as a result no one gave us much of anything. For the next few days we would be living in a tent, if we were lucky. A surprise however was that one of the units was on a mission and we could use their hooch, at least temporarily until we built our own. Our days were filled with instruction on the use of the boats and outboard motors. These boats were nothing more than troop carriers made out of fiberglass with an outboard motor. Any idiot could learn to drive them—that is until we lost a motor because one of our idiots forgot to clamp the outboard on the boat! These boats were death traps, they had no armament and would immediately sink when holed by a single well-placed shot. After a few days we were really getting bored because of the constant repetition of our duties. Sgt. Carver saw this and put us to work filling sand bags to put around the fuel storage tanks. If nothing else this passed the time.

There was no way to keep beer or soda cold and the drinking water was very nasty. To make matters worse the unit in whose hooch we were living was returning soon so we had to do something.

The next morning at breakfast in the mess tent I spotted a friendly face, Sgt. Cook. He was one of the people on the plane from Maguire with me. He was the mess Sergeant of this outfit and we immediately exchanged greetings. From that point on our little unit had the run of the mess tent, anytime day or night.

Boredom was setting in so we were ordered to start building our own accommodations. This seemed just the thing to do. We would love to build our own hooch but didn't know how. The other problem we had was that there wasn't any solid ground. The only available places were right in the middle of rice paddies. Fortunately we were attached to the 15th Engineers and they solved these minor problems.

Using a pickaxe, holes were punched in the bottom sides of six 55-gallon drums. This allowed them to fill with water to the level of the paddy. The drums were set and arranged in a 15x25 rectangle. Placed on top of the drums were 4x4s, forming a base upon which to build a solid floor. Screening was stapled to the bottom side of the floor preventing infestation by mosquitoes from the paddy itself. From that point on, it was a piece of cake to build walls and screen them also, install roof joists, a tent roof and finally a screen door. In one or two days we had our "hooch", and believe it or not, it was a cozy place to live.

DATE: 11/15/1967
TIME: 0700 HRS.
LOCATION:AN NHUT TAN, SMALL VILLAGE
SOUTHWEST OF TAN TRU

"TRY TO REMEMBER THOSE DAYS IN . . . ."

One clear day in early November there was much activity on the part of the infantry troops. They were going on a mission to a place a few klicks south of where we were. They would occupy a village called An Nhut Tan, a secure village that would be used as the base of operations. All of us were so bored that we volunteered to go. We took four boats with us. We left via the "jolly green giant", a Chinook helicopter that ferried us for the short ride. We flew because the area around An Nhut Tan was infested with Victor Charlie and their activity made everyone nervous. There was a particular place on the river below An Nhut Tan nicknamed "the testicles". The river twisted into a sack, turned sharply and doubled back on itself. The area of land where it almost met was great for ambushes, and the VC readily accommodated us. After you were attacked on one side, it would take a few minutes for the boats to go around the bend in the river. The gooks would cross the short distance of land, set up, and then attack again. No amount of artillery or gunships seemed to stop them from repeating their ambushes day after day. It was very frustrating! They had you by the scrotum, hence the name!

We landed further on up the river at An Nhu Tan. This was a crossroads of canals that was used in former days as a collection point for the rice harvest. There was a large drying shed that was empty, so we slung hammocks to sleep since it had a large roof that kept out the rain. Almost immediately we were inundated with kids.

At this point in our tenure with the 9th Division, our contact with the enemy was light. This was going to change shortly and forever change our attitude about the VC. We used only one of the boats, so rather than just sit around, a few of us volunteered to go on a recon mission with an infantry platoon. The previous night another platoon was ambushed and took some casualties. We would investigate the area to see if the enemy had left anything behind. The only thing we found were a few shell casings from an AK-47, two spider holes, enemy foxholes, and a length of wire that was used to detonate a claymore mine. When we got back to An Nhut Tan we learned that we would be going back to Tan Tru in a day or two. I volunteered to hand carry a set of orders back to Tan Tru. I delivered the orders, and a half hour later was back in An Nhut Tan. What we didn't know was that according to intelligence, the VC was planning a large attack on our base at Tan Tru, and all were needed to defend it.

DATE: 11/16/1967
TIME: 1400 HRS.
LOCATION: TAN TRU

"HOME SWEET HOME . . . THIS WEEK"

It was almost a pleasure to get back to our hooch, even though we still had to put the finishing touches on it. Most of us were tired and we wanted to catch some ZZZs. Early that evening the artillery unit was called, for a fire mission. We could see the flashes in the distance but could only hear them firing, not landing. The next day we were assigned to upgrade and expand the bunkers. This entailed filling more sandbags.

We finally got mail; it had been almost two months since my arrival in country, no airboats and no mail. The reason for not getting any mail was that we moved around and were never settled in one place for longer than a few weeks. There were four letters and the hometown newspaper, The Independent Press. One letter was from my folks, and the other three were from my girlfriend, Barbara. I was very anxious because I had not received a letter from her in a very long time. She had broken up with me and gotten married a few weeks after we graduated high school. A year and a half later we got back together. We started seeing each other just before I left for Vietnam; what can I say, I was "in love". When I wrote to her, the letters were sent to her address at work. She was fine and missed me very much. Please be careful and don't do anything stupid, she would write. She also said she was getting a divorce. Her words were music to my ears, something that I could look forward to. Reading her letters took my mind off my current situation, if only for a little while. The letter from my folks was hilarious. It was now the middle of November, and a mission south into "Indian country" was in the offing. No specifics were given other than to get the boats ready. The mission was going to be in couple of days. I guess the Intel was wrong about the attack on Tan Tru

One of the few things that made us smile was that we were awarded the Combat Infantry Badge for our actions against the enemy at An NhuTan.

DATE: 11/17/1967
TIME: 0500 HR
LOCATION: OUR HOOCH IN TAN TRU

"HEY! THE ALARM DIDN'T GO OFF!"

We were abruptly awakened at 0500 HRS. not by a screaming sergeant, but by a VC mortar attack. I scrambled to get my weapon, my flack vest, and my helmet. It was totally dark and you can imagine the chaos. I was out of the hooch running toward the nearest bunker, following Harry Walton when a mortar round landed 6 or 7 feet behind me. The blast knocked me over and I rolled into a somersault, got up and kept on running, finally making it to the bunker. Upon entering and trying to catch my breath, I felt sweat running down my back on one side. The only problem was it wasn't sweat, it was blood. I had sustained a shrapnel wound and didn't even feel it, no pain whatsoever. Harry and a medic were there and immediately placed a bandage on it to stop the bleeding. After the attack I went to the medical personnel and had the wound properly cleaned and bandaged. The wound did not seem to be serious, but I had to change the bandage twice a day and keep it dry. Gun shot wounds could not be stitched up, but had to heal from the inside out. The Doc also told me "YOU NOW HAVE A PURPLE HEART! GREAT! I was in country for two months plus a few days, and now I get wounded, not even bad enough to get out of the field.

The next day my stupidity again raised its ugly head. The entire company was going out on a mission to the south, deep in the delta. Because I was wounded, I could stay behind, but we were a unit and all of us wanted to stick together, so I insisted I was able to go. We traveled with our whaleboats, strapped underneath the, "jolly green giant", Chinook helicopter to an old bombed out plantation complex located far to the south deep in the delta, or affectionately known as "Indian country".

DATE: 11/18/67
TIME: MIDDAY
LOCATION: PLANTATION COMPLEX, SOUTH OF
             TAN TRU

I'VE BEEN IN WORSE PLACES . . .
OH YEA! WHERE?

Two canals converged on each other forming a cross. The plantation complex was on one of the corners. There were no roads around us, only the canal on two sides and large rice paddies on the other side and to the front. These paddies were adjacent to each other and three or four more were further extended out in each direction. In the distance you could see a small bombed out village which had been abandoned. The village was destroyed either by air or ground troops weeks before. We did not need all of the boats that were brought so we were assigned other duties. An artillery unit was choppered in with many supplies as well. Toward evening when it was still light, I was assigned to perimeter guard. This was going to be a "pain in the ass", as I had to lay propped up on a dike with the lower half of my body in a rice paddy. My position was on the corner of the paddy with a short timer named Sgt. Frank Otto, from the 2/60th. He was from California and couldn't wait to get back home. He had a week to go before leaving the country, but as a Platoon Sgt. He felt he had an obligation to his people, and to us, as we were fairly new. I told him he was nuts!

As the evening grew into night and we were talking he noticed the weapon I was using was an M-79 grenade launcher. He immediately started to curse. Alarmed I asked what was wrong. He just looked at me and said," I hope they don't attack us tonight". I again asked why? He then answered that we both had M-79 grenade launchers which were ineffective in rice paddies, as the shrapnel would not spray out in water. To make matters worse we only had two shotgun rounds each. I immediately became concerned and hoped they wouldn't attack us either as "I was not the best hand to hand combat trained soldier in the army". Needless to say we were a bit uneasy.

About 2 A.M. the villa started to get mortared. Earlier that afternoon they had airlifted a battery of 155 howitzers, and obviously the enemy had wanted to put them out of action. On the perimeter we could see the flashes from the enemy mortars. Both of us were ordered to shoot a few rounds at the flashes that were coming from the burned out village. We did so and got off about 3 or 4 rounds apiece. No sooner had we fired our rounds when a VC 50 cal. machine gun opened up and we were forced to keep our heads down, while we fertilized the paddies. We could see the tracers about a foot over our heads (it seemed like 2 inches), as they were trying to get the guys who shot at them as well as the artillery personnel. All of a sudden two helicopter gunships arrived and began a little raking of their own. The gunships fired on the enemy positions and then turned to go around for a second run. The VC fired up at the gunships. Coming around they again devastated the area, and again the gooks fired up at them. After rocketing and mini gunning the area for a third time, the shooting stopped, and all was quiet except for the coming and going of other choppers. There must have been some wounded because there was a couple of dustoffs landing and taking off. I hoped that no one in our unit was hit. A little later we were reinforced on the perimeter and this caused us to breathe a little easier. We learned that luckily no one in our unit was hit. Finally after a long and scary night, morning came and I welcomed it with joy. We could finally dry out, as we were well marinated from lying in the rice paddy all night.

DATE: 11/19/1967
TIME: 0630 HRS
LOCATION: A RICE PADDY DIKE, ON THE PERIMETER
OF THE PLANTATION

"HEY HUMPHREY, LEECHES SUCK . . . LITERALLY!"

I felt an itch on my leg and reached down to scratch it only to feel something long and slimy. I started yelling and jumping about when Sgt. Otto grabbed me and told me to calm down. He told me to take my pants off, and in doing so, I saw that there were long green slimy leeches from my crotch to my calves down to my ankles. I was on the verge of freaking out until I saw him nonchalantly remove his pants, and he was covered as well. Shades of Bogart in the African Queen! I then received instructions on leach removal. We lit two cigarettes and stood on the dike burning leaches off each other. They are an amazing animal; they suck your blood and become elongated, sometimes a foot long. When you touch them with a cigarette, they immediately contract to an inch or two long, let go and fall off. Their bite continues to bleed but only for a short time after they fall off. Their bite is also in the shape of a peace sign; it makes you wonder if the peace sign was designed to extol "blood sucking leaches". Returning to our foxholes on the dry side of the villa, after the pleasant experience I just had, the howitzers had a fire mission. We were just passing in front of them when they fired. I thought that my eardrums where blown out as the unexpected blast knocked Rumsey and me into a world of deafness. All we could hear for a few hours was constant ringing along with a dull ache. Fortunately our hearing returned later and we could again hear the "the Doors" broadcast on AFVN.

DATE: 11/21/1967
TIME: DAYTIME
LOCATION: TAN TRU, NORTH OF RICE PLANTATION

"ON THE ROAD AGAIN AND AGAIN"

After two days of no enemy activity, the mission was over, and we returned to Tan Tru, still waiting for our boats to arrive. For the next couple of weeks we continued to do local operations in and around Tan Tru. There was a village-clearing job downstream that was a suspected VC supply depot. The only problem was that to get to the village, you again had to go through "the testicles". No matter how much artillery or air support you called in, Charley still managed to clean your clock. It was getting really tiresome. No matter what we did, like hemorrhoids, they were always there to give you a pain in the ass. This went on another two weeks when thankfully our airboats arrived from the states, and we were ordered back to Bearcat.

By this time the First Airboat Platoon had completed their training and there was some controversy on who would get the boats. Our platoon won out however, but sergeant Caughlin was reassigned to the first platoon.

VIGNETTE 4: KIDS, KIDS, KIDS

"AND THE CHILDREN WERE NESTLED ALL SNUG . . . NOT"

The one thing you could definitely count on in Viet Nam is that no matter where you would go, children would always show up. They are the true future of VN. From their smiles and constant chatter, you don't realize what they go through in their daily lives. It is not very difficult to get close to them as we learned one hot and dusty day.

Our airboats hadn't come in from the States yet so we were assigned to a unit that used whaleboats mainly for transporting troops across canals. The place was called Tan Tru. It was a small base camp near a small village and there was some Viet Cong activity. We befriended a small boy whose parents were killed earlier that year. This kid was named Thamy (Tommy). He could speak English pretty good, and we took him under our wings. He would clean up our hooch, take our dirty clothes to be cleaned by some mama-san, sweep out and around our bunks, shine our boots, and would get us needed items when asked. He quickly became indispensable. He liked to talk and he would tell us stories about himself and his family. Sometimes he would talk hushed tones and tears would accompany this. His father was a village chief and when the Viet Cong came they wanted the rice that the villagers just harvested. His father refused, and as a result he watched while his pregnant wife was beaten and raped. He still refused and was summarily executed. Little kids should not ever be subjected to these horrors, yet this was almost an everyday occurrence in Vietnam. The VC ruled by terror. Thamy seemed like a normal kid but did have his quiet moments; you would wonder what wheels were turning in his head.

A few days later we went on another mission to a place called An Nhut Tan. We set up shop in an open-air warehouse and the first thing that surrounded us was, you guessed it, kids! Everywhere we would go, kids appeared like magic.

After four or five weeks our airboats arrived and we had to leave. As we packed our gear onto the trucks that would take us back to Bearcat, we avoided eye contact with Thamy. I knew that we would never see him again. It was very hard for us to leave him especially when he kept asking us "where are we going" and could he come with us.

Life for orphans sucks in Vietnam, but we hoped that it in the future it would be better for him. We had arranged with the mess sergeant to look out for him. As we drove away I hoped he would survive intact and prayed that we would win this war for his sake if nothing more.

Every place we went after that we never again allowed the children to get close to us. We gave them food, candy, clothes, but always in the back of our minds, mine especially, was Thamy. Whether it was with the Thais at Long Than or the bridge on the Dong Nai River, the kids were everywhere.

There was no point, we are here today and moved to someplace else the next, so it made life easier for all of us. Yes, we made friends with the kids; yes, we gave them food and candy, bought things they were selling; yes we provided medical help for cuts and bruises, but we would always try to keep this cool façade of detachment. I said we tried, and if you believe this crock, then I guess that you still believe in Santa Claus! These kids were a large part of humanity in an inhumane war; to ignore them or their plight was against all you believed in. To completely walk away from them, you had to be a cold-hearted, uncaring bastard, and thank God none of us fit into that category. The French have a saying for situations where little can be done and that is "C'est la vie!" Such is life! Such is life indeed.

DATE: 12/4/67
TIME: 1000 HRS
LOCATION: CAMP BEARCAT, NORTHEAST OF
        SAIGON

"THIS IS FUBAR, THERE'S ALWAYS A SNAFU"

As stated earlier, our Airboats had arrived in country but had not yet been delivered to Bearcat. This gave us time to relax and enjoy the use the base facilities. We would go to the PX to buy cameras and watches, which we were, always losing, buy film or get it developed, eat ice cream and hamburgers and to send letters home.

My wound was starting to bother me, as the shrapnel seemed to be bulging out under my arm. I saw the Doc and he said he could remove it under a local anesthetic. He first wanted an x-ray to see if there was any more shrapnel floating around. After checking the film, he told me I was very lucky as the shrapnel bounced off my rib bone and was diverted from my heart to my side, pushing the skin out. This was very sobering—to think I could have been killed! He removed the shrapnel; he bragged it was his first operation, I think he was really a dentist, and he wanted to keep it, but so did I and I won, now I have a nice souvenir.

We were hanging around Bearcat for a couple of weeks. It became apparent that the army didn't know what to do with us. We were also moved from one barracks to another, not knowing to whom or where we would be assigned. It really didn't bother us except for the fact nobody seemed to want us.

At the end of November or the beginning of December we were assigned to E company 15th Engineering Bn., for rations, quarters and administration. They had the 5-ton flat bed trucks to transport the air boats to water as well as the crane to unload us. Most of us were infantry, retrained as Airboat Pilots, and now we are working with the engineers! What a cluster fuck!

VIGNETTE 5:
DESCRIPTION OF AIRBOAT

"1 BOAT, 2 BOATS, 3 BOATS A DOLLAR"

The Airboat was dark green in color, made out of fiberglass and was about sixteen feet long by four and a half feet wide. The cockpit had a molded plastic seat with the control panel on the right. On the left was the control for the vanes or fins which turned the boat left or right. On either side of the seat were two self-sealing twenty-gallon gas tanks. The gas we used was JP-4, aviation fuel. Directly in back of the seat and raised to about head level was the engine, enveloped by a metal screen which protected one from the propeller. The engine itself was a Lycoming four cylinder and was also used in small piper cubs. On the front of the boat was a gun mount on which could fit either .50 cal machine gun or an M-60 machine gun. When the boats arrived they had .50 cal. Machine guns on them. We later found out that it was downright impracticable to use these weapons. The ammo added too much weight, reducing speed. The recoil of the fifties would, when moving at maximum speed, would throw the boat on its side. We ended up using M-60's.

The boat was painted a dark camouflage green. The fiberglass surrounded Styrofoam in the front thus making the boats light as possible. In fact these boats were so light and thin skinned that a BB would have an easy time of going through them. The boats were manufactured by the Hurricane Fibreglass Co. Aircat Division in Hallandale FL.

DATE: 12/16/1967
TIME: 1200 HRS
LOCATION: RUNG SAT, EAST OF SAIGON

"PIRATES OF PENZANCE . . . NOT!"

The U.S. had a number of allies who fought beside us in Vietnam. One of those units was the Queens Cobra Regiment of the Royal Thai Army.

It was decided that the Thai's, (Royal Thai Army) area of responsibility would be in the "Rung Sat Special Zone, southeast of Saigon. This was an inaccessible area except by boats. It was a dense forest of Mangroves and a maze of waterways ideal for Airboats to operate in. The VC had always operated here with impunity and always at night. Rung Sat means forest of assassins and had been used by Vietnamese pirates throughout the history of Indochina. This area of waterways was extremely well suited for the tactics used by the VC.

In assigning the Thais to this AO, the 15th Engineers were helping them to build a small base camp from which to launch operations throughout the zone. They were using a very large machine called the tree crusher to clear an area 75 yards from the camp. It became hopelessly mired in mud, later to be surrounded by the incoming tide . . .

DATE: 12/18/1967
TIME: 2330 HRS
LOCATION: LONG THANH, SOUTHEAST OF SAIGON

"THE PROVERBIAL SOUNDS OF
SNEAKING AROUND"

The big machine that was used to crush and mangle any vegetation it rolled over got stuck and was submerged under water, or at least half of it was. Earlier the Tree Crusher had been clearing out a perimeter area around the Thai camp. It had cleared an area about 75 yards from the first line of barb wire and was proceeding to widen this zone when all of a sudden it became stuck in the tidal mud. It could no longer move.

The Tree Crusher was designed to be amphibious and should not be affected by water. It was electrically operated, but there was one tiny design flaw. The air intake was located under the operators cab and very close to the ground. It started to suck in water and mud. Not realizing too, was that the tide was out and in a couple of hours the machine would be surrounded by water. This combination of brackish water and mud shorted out the motors and engines. These ugly circumstances caused the first real mission for the Second Airboat Plt. That mission was to provide security for the Tree Crusher and the crew of engineers that were deployed to free it.

About 100 yards from where it was stuck was a perfect launching site for our airboats. The trucks could pull within a few feet of the muddy waterway where we could be lifted by a small truck crane and placed gently on the water. As the tide came in we could be deployed in and around the vicinity of the Tree Crusher.

During the day there was no problem, but nighttime was a different story. We were all scared of the night because that was the time that the enemy was active, and all of us were very wary about that which we did not know. It took us a while to realize that the night time was also our friend, and before long we welcomed it also.

Meanwhile back to the Tree Crusher. We formed an ambush perimeter all around to protect it. If you imagine holding up your hand and spreading your fingers, the TC was stuck right in the "V" of the pointer and index finger. The spaces in between the fingers are the streams that embrace the land or what there is of it. The area between the thumb and pointer was the launching site we used to put our boats into the water. The perimeter we formed into an arc from the pinkie to the thumb with two boats positioned at the TC. My boat was the farthest out and we had just settled into our prearranged position. Our boats could only carry three Americans including the driver, and still maintain our top speed. BZ, Dan, and I had just tied up the boat at our position and prepared ourselves for the long night ahead of us. Sleep was one commodity that eluded all of us, so we talked to each other in very low hushed tones as voices could carry for miles. As the night grew deeper, star shells in the distance were lighting up the sky. We hunkered down lower in our boats, as the fingers of light from the illumination rounds seemed to reach out and touch us, baring our souls and location for all to see. As the flares floated slowly and gently to earth, eerie shadows reached out to grab us, and pull us back to the dark. Thankfully the light soon disappeared behind the mangroves far away. The quiet returned, and I lapsed into thoughts of home. I suddenly realized that it would soon be Christmas and it had been almost a year since I received my draft notice. Time flies when you are having fun. Soon after that, it would be my birthday, on the 6th of February, I would be 22. Who would have thought a year ago I would be sitting in an airboat in the middle of a stinking mangrove swamp in Viet Nam.

I was interrupted from my thoughts when I thought I heard some movement in back of us. I gently woke the others and we all listened intently. CRACK! A branch or twig had broken, and for sure something was moving in back of us. As quietly as possible I radioed the TC that someone or something was moving to our rear. It was between the Thai base camp and us. The message was passed on to the camp and all the boats were ordered to come back to the TC. That order couldn't have come fast enough for me, and before you could say "DINKEY DAU", we started our engine and drove back to the Tree Crusher.

No sooner had we returned and secured the boats, then "all hell broke loose"—tracer bullets flew into the camp and explosions were going off very close to us. I wondered if fiberglass would stop a bullet, knowing we had very little protection. After a few minutes we realized that we weren't the targets but the Thai base camp was, so we breathed a little easier. We knew that the enemy was between the camp and us, a perfect crossfire, and we began to open up on the location where the tracers were coming from. I moved to the front of my boat. We had a 50 cal. Machine gun and I began firing; we had been experimenting earlier with this gun and found that you couldn't fire it while moving, as the recoil could capsize the boat. When the boat was stationary however, it was fine. Everyone was shooting! This lasted a few minutes when we received a call to stop all weapons as our bullets were also going into the camp. We were allowed to shoot only if we were attacked or if we had sure targets. Bullets were also flying past our heads from the compound so we were forced to keep low. We hugged the deck the rest of the night, and just before dawn the firing ceased.

The casualties suffered by the Thais were unbelievably low; no one killed, and only four wounded. The VC however suffered many dead; at least 30 bodies were found and many blood trails leading off in every direction. I guess my earlier call alerted everyone that something was going down and to get ready. The Thais captured many weapons, both crew served and personal. It was amazing that the enemy suffered so much of a loss and the good guys hardly any.

The next day broke bright and clear and there was no trace of the firefight the night before. We were ordered to stay where we were until the engineers decided what to do. During the next few days we reconnoitered the area. The winding waterways were like mazes. We eventually found our way around going through them so many times. These routes and waterways became imbedded in your memory. It would take us weeks and even then you couldn't be sure. We had to remember everything double—when the tide was in, as well as when it was out. The tides were awesome because the rivers and streams were 100 to 150 feet wide at high tide and only 5 to 10 feet wide at low tide. The fluctuation from high to low tide was about 13 feet. The one positive of this was that no one cared. Our boats could go just as good on mud as in water

After a few days the Engineers decided to tow the Tree Crusher down river to firmer ground. Again we had to guard this floating monstrosity during its journey. It was pretty easy to float the TC, and then tow it to a stream. The Engineers had huge rubber pontoons which were solidly fixed to the huge machine. Once this was done it was simple enough to tow it down river to more solid landing spaces where trucks could be brought in for the disassembly. We patrolled back and forth between the floating Tree Crusher as it was being towed to its final destination. There was no enemy activity. It was a trip of about six kilometers. Once this mission was completed, our boats were loaded onto the trucks and back to Bearcat we went. Now that the TC was on solid ground, an infantry unit took over security for it as it took another day to dismantle, put it onto trucks, and take it back to Bearcat for repair. We also heard that the Bob Hope show was coming to Bearcat and we all wanted to see it, so we were doubly glad to get back.

VIGNETTE 6: MANGROVES

"... A TREE WHOSE HUNGRY MOUTH
IS PRESSED ..."

The area southeast of Saigon is called the Rung Sat. This swamp is filled with a myriad of waterways and streams that are like a maze with no path leading out.

The indigenous flora is mangrove which allows no other kind to grow and thrives in brackish water. This tangled morass of vegetation is so entwined that one cannot take a step without slipping or falling into thick stinking mud. It is ideal for a determined enemy to hide completely and avoid detection. This has been so for centuries as Vietnamese pirates and thieves have always used it.

This whole area is tidal and it is amazing. When the tide is in, the water engulfs and embraces the mangroves so it looks as if the plants grow right out of the water. It was as if they grew in a large lake. When the tide goes out, the water disappears into tiny rivulets 3 or 4 meters wide. The tidal fluctuation was 12 to 14 ft. The enemy used floating platforms to store supplies and to sleep.

When the tide went out, vast mud flats that smelled of rotting vegetation would appear and were populated by zillions of mudskippers. These fishlike amphibians were in and out of their burrows as danger or mates appeared. These burrows were left to either bake in the afternoon sun or bathe in the steamy moonlight of the night, giving the appearance of a pock marked landscape. This wet and muddy land is ideal for airboats, and airboats were the way for us to penetrate an area that was ceded to the Viet Cong since French rule. It was no longer inaccessible, but it sure as hell was still inhospitable.

During the day fishing boats and sampans carrying rice and other goods traveled these waterways, but at sundown everything stopped and disappeared. It was totally inhabited and controlled by the VC. It was a "free fire zone", and that meant that anything that moved was the enemy. Enemy supplies were moved at night, their personnel were moved to other areas, and most of the attacks on our installations would begin here. After those attacks they retreated into this swamp because they knew no one could follow. Rung Sat, meaning "forest of assassins" was aptly named. Into this venue was thrust the Second Airboat Platoon, 9TH Inf. Div and the Royal Thai Army.

Our pocket patch was an inverted triangle with a small airboat below the letters WAR. These letters stood for W, water, A, assault and R, recon. This acronym couldn't have been more appropriate. All of these functions were carried out by our platoon. During the day we would reconnoiter areas that we felt would make good ambush sights. Sometimes we would stop and search sampans and sometimes even helped fisherman by throwing concussion grenades into the water and watch as the stunned fish floated to the surface for easy retrieval. At night we would go out in groups of 5 or 6 boats, tie up in the position we had scoped out earlier, and wait for the enemy to come by. Although our boats were very loud, you still couldn't tell exactly where. The sound came from everywhere, and unless you actually saw us, you couldn't be sure where we where. We became very irritating to the Cong, and we loved it.

Try as they might the enemy had a problem shooting and hitting us because we moved so fast. We traveled at 40 mph, over water and mud. I was recently talking to Mark Kizzire from the wilds of Oregon, and he put it very succinctly "We really sterilized the Rung Sat". In fact, the VC no longer had free reign over this area while we operated there.

The only time we were vulnerable was when our speed was compromised. This was never more evident than April 10, 1968, when we suffered our first loss of life.

VIGNETTE 7: MOSQUITOES

"AND A PESTILANCE WAS UPON THE LAND"

Malaria was a huge problem for the military. It was also a big problem for me . . . I did not want to be the recipient of some infected mosquito's saliva.

When we arrived in country along with our uniforms, boots, weapons, helmet, and flak vests, we were also issued mosquito netting. Once shown how to use this item, we were also instructed that this is as important to you as your weapon. I thought this was a rather overblown statement until I realized that it was no joke!! We also were issued spray cans and plastic bottles of insect repellant. The soft brimmed jungle hats came with a net, and again it didn't take long to wonder why.

The next part of the indoctrination on malaria was the issuance of the hated malaria pill. It was not only issued to you, but the officers and NCOs stood and watched while you took it. These pills were to be taken once a week without fail, or you would get an article 15. They were big and orange, about the size of a nickel and twice as thick. After you took them, you felt queasy for a couple of hours, and made frequent trips to the latrine, with the shizzles and drits. This was not a pleasant experience. After taking the pill for a few weeks, you tended to find something else to do, even volunteering for unsavory details, anything to avoid taking it.

When we began working with the Thais, the need for the netting was without question. The mosquitoes were so thick at night that you would grab a handful of air, open your hand, and there would be 20 or 30 dead skeeters. Any area on your body that was not covered or slathered with repellant was attacked with a vengeance. These mosquitoes were masters of finding the tiniest of openings and proceeded to feed on us "red-blooded American" boys. Once we acknowledged that they were a formidable enemy, we gave them no quarter, or I should say no open or bare skin to attack.

Getting back to the pill, many of us did not take it, although we pretended to, me included. I would also note that those of us who did not take the pill did not get malaria. Most of the people that did take the pill seemed to get malaria. Were we lucky?

At night when you slept, you made sure that the netting was closed and sealed. If you didn't use the net at night, you woke up in the morning with giant, welts, and that was unpleasant and very itchy. When you went on ambushes at night you used your jungle hat with the net. On all the exposed parts of your body you bathed in repellent but tried to keep its use to a minimum and never used it on your face. The bug juice burned when it got into your eyes. It got there not by touching but by sweat running into them, and you always sweat. After a while mosquito care became no more of an annoyance than drying and caring for your feet. It became something that you did automatically, like cleaning your weapon or letting your feet dry out.

DATE: 12/23/1967
TIME: 1100 HRS.
LOCATION: CAMP BEARCAT, EAST OF SAIGON

"THANKS FOR THE MEMORIES . . . ."

The Christmas holidays were spent at Bearcat, and it was not bad. The Bob Hope show was scheduled for that afternoon, and we were certainly looking forward to it, so were 20, 000 other G.I.'s, and space was at a premium. Our area in Bearcat was pretty close to where the show was so no one hurried, which was our mistake. All of the space around the stage was taken, and we were relegated to the rear area in back of the crowd. Even at this, the show was great. Raquel Welch was with Bob, and the jokes were hilarious. Miss World was there as were many of her compatriots. Les Brown and his band of renown were there. It seemed as if all the soldiers in the 9th were there too. Raquel Welch and Miss World (Miss Peru) were the first round-eyed women we had seen in a long time, and it was a hoot. The show lasted until late afternoon and when it was over we were the first to get out, though a few members lagged behind. I later found out that as the troupe was going to the jeeps that would take them to the choppers, one member of our platoon, who shall remain nameless, was very close to Raquel Welch and grabbed her ass. As Raquel was surrounded by a thousand guys she kept looking around at the offending soldier but couldn't tell who it was. I know it really pissed her off, but what a story this airboat pilot has.

As we were walking up the road; I got a good shot of Bob but in doing so was almost run over by his driver. We could see them board their choppers for a trip to another base to do another show.

I don't care what anyone says, but for a man to give up most of his Christmas's to be with GI's in a war zone is pretty terrific, and for sure there will be a place in heaven for him.

That night we all went to the battalion mess hall and had a real Christmas dinner with all the trimmings, even if it was out of a thermos like container. Jason Bitela who earlier had volunteered for KP was grinning like a Cheshire cat. We all thought he was crazy to volunteer in the first place but soon realized that we were the losers. In volunteering Jason was assigned to serve, you guessed it, Bob Hope and his entourage. He had his picture taken with Bob Hope with Hope's arm around him, as well as a photo with Raquel Welch. I guess we were the jerks and not Jason.

It was a short-lived respite, however, because the next day we were scheduled to go back to the Thais at their base camp at Long Thanh.

DATE: 12/30/1967
TIME: 0900 HRS.
LOCATION: RUNG SAT AT LONG THANH, SOUTHEAST
OF SAIGON

"OH JOY! OH JOY! OH JOY OF JOYS!"

After our successful debut it was decided that we would be permanently based at the Thai base camp along with our boats.

Our sleeping accommodations were non-existent until we got a few tents from the engineers. We also would have to fill sandbags for the walls. You couldn't dig very deep in the ground because the water table was so high. In fact to get water to take a bath, you only had to dig a foot down and the hole would fill with water. Unfortunately, tent living offered almost no protection from any mortar attacks, so we would have to build a bunker big enough for us to live in. We also had to make some sort of revetments (bunker) for our boats, as we just left them in the open, inviting the enemy to destroy them.

The engineers built a wooden shell of a building, which we would later learn would be covered with sandbags. This would be our bunker and home for however long we would be here.

Our first kill was just before the TET Offensive. Five boats had been out on an ambush position and a lone gook in a sampan came rowing into their sights.

Unfortunately for him was he was seen before seeing them. The 2nd Airboat platoon's first confirmed kill. We all celebrated the action, even with "Luke the Gook". We took turns taking pictures with Luke, propped up between two of us, with a cigarette in his mouth and a can of beer in his hand and his glasses on, with his guts popping out. When we were done we buried him near his thirty compatriots who died at the hands of the Thais a couple of days before.

This is an accurate description of how war can really depersonalize and desensitize human beings. At the time we thought it was a hoot! Looking back, I wondered how we could ever do something like this.

VIGNETTE 8:
ART OF SANDBAG FILLING

"OOH! AAH! THAT'S THE SOUND OF THE MEN . . . ."

It was decided that we would have to build our own luxury accommodations, again! Being expert hooch builders we all figured no problem until we found out we had to build a massive bunker. We were alone in the boonies and subject to constant mortar rocket and ground attack. The bunker was to be surrounded with sandbags, how many we didn't know, filled by us.

Upon completion of the inner shell which was built out of 2x8s and 2x4s with plywood walls, covered in tar paper. We started covering and surrounding it with sandbags. The task of filling sandbags became the thing we did every waking hour of every day, except for missions. It was a real challenge to keep at it seven days a week, but it had to be done. We got a break because the engineers brought in a bulldozer to dig a mass grave for the dead VC that was killed earlier in battle. As they were going our Lt. Stone asked if they could push up sand around the bunker shell they had built. They could only push sand halfway up the sides, as it would collapse if any more pressure were applied. Just this, however, saved us from filling many more bags. They also scraped out a pit for our boats and again the filling of sandbags was a little easier. We still had to fill mucho bags for the roof as well as one wall where the entrance was. The bunker became known as the Pyramid; it was really a towering achievement and we all felt fairly safe from a mortar attack while sleeping in it. We now had only to fill about 10,000 bags instead of 20,000. The whole project took all of a month and a half to be finished. We worked on filling sandbags during the day and went out in our boats on night ambushes. Upon returning, we filled more sand bags. When did we get sleep? well there was a few hours in between, which did suffice. Since the day that we were mortared at Tan Tru and I got wounded, I wanted our bunker finished or least mortar-proofed. This was our main motivation, or I should say mine.

Our Platoon would have made Henry Ford proud as we had developed an assembly line to fill the bags. Some of us would shovel sand into a hopper, some of us would insure the sand kept on flowing, others held the bag open while it filled; we then would pass it to the tying experts, who would pass it to the carriers who would strategically place it on the bunker. Wade Nail had come up with this great idea. After about a month we finally finished. We were so happy we had a party. If we only knew that a few weeks later we would be moved out to another locale, the bunker would be bulldozed and blown up; would we still have been in a party mode? HELL YES!!! We always liked parties, no matter what the occasion or time of day or night.

DATE: 1/18/1968
TIME: 1400 HRS
LOCATION: RUNG SAT

"A SHITTY DAY FOR RICH!"

It was January 18th, and that morning there was a briefing. We were to take out some Thai infantry and drop them off in one location, move to another, and hopefully the Thais would push the enemy toward us. The mission was uneventful, and as the boats were returning to base, Lt. Stone said that Red Field's boat and Rich Rumsey's boat were to follow him. Rich relates part of the story from here.

"Lt. Stone said that he was going to show the Thai officers how the boats operated. We followed him and turned up this small canal finding it very narrow. We traveled up until we saw a tree that fell across blocking our way. Stone signaled to turn around and go back out. We complied and Red was now first in line, I was in the middle, then Lt.Stone in the rear. Red went back down the canal when a claymore was set off directly at my boat. The VC had set up an ambush my boat was the main target. Everyone on my boat was wounded INCLUDING ME! I was hit in the leg knocking me out of my seat. I managed to get up to and fire my M-16."

Stone, with the Thai officers, went by the disabled boat firing on the ambush positions. One of the Thai officers was wounded, and Lt. Stone felt he should get them to safety. At this point Rumsey was severely wounded a second time but managed to fire a couple of M-79 rounds. He managed to get into the seat but was wounded a third time. At the same time a FAC, forward air controller, in a "birddog" saw his predicament and fired two rockets on the enemy position. The firing stopped, and Rich managed to regain the seat and proceeded to get the boat back to our lagoon. Rich blacked out and drove the boat into some trees, and the branches slapping him in the face brought Rich to. We turned the boat back into the channel. Rich couldn't operate the steering as my arm was bleeding severely but one of the Thais operated it for him.

Rich, although severely wounded, brought his boat with the wounded Thais back to the canal entrance where other boats saw his predicament and helped him land the boat safely. Red didn't even know that the others were ambushed until Lt. Stone arrived with the Thai officers. Rich was awarded the Silver Star for his heroism and saving the lives of the wounded Thais.

DATE: 1/25/1968
TIME: 2100 HRS.
PLACE: THAI BASE CAMP, LONG THANH

"ANOTHER SHITTY DAY, THIS TIME FOR RED!"

A few days later we were sitting around in small groups drinking, playing cards or bullshitting when the Thais received a fire mission from one of their patrols. We all took notice and were watching and listening to the mortars being fired, then landing on the unseen enemy positions. The distinctive "Whumpf" of the rounds being fired was broken by a puffy whiney sound. We all looked toward the mortar and saw a group running to aide someone who was standing near the gun. It was "Red" Fields. He was a bloody mess and had a field dressing on his head. A mortar shell had misfired and only shot a short distance out of the tube, hitting Red on the head and cracking open his skull. He was conscious but disoriented. We called in a "dustoff"and had him evacuated to a hospital in Bearcat. We later learned that he was evacuated to the States for more intensive care.

This was the first case a member of the platoon suffered a casualty by friendly fire. It was one thing to be shot by the enemy, but being hurt in an accident had a sobering effect on us all.

DATE: 1/29/1968
TIME: 1500 HRS
LOCATION: THAI BASE CAMP AT LONG THANH,
SOUTHEAST OF SAIGON

"HAPPY NEW YEAR! VIETNAMESE STYLE!"

The most important holiday in Vietnam is Tet or the lunar New Year. Every Vietnamese returns to their birthplace to celebrate with their families. It is a time of great celebration. There was a truce declared but the VC would ignore this and show their brutality throughout the country.

The attack on the Thais was the precursor of the Tet Offensive. Every large base and even the U.S. Embassy were attacked. At our base we only received a few mortar rounds; most of the action was at Bearcat, Long Binh, and the rest of the major cities. We temporarily suspended missions but remained on alert in the camp. We were ordered to resume operations and to set up ambush positions at night along the navigable waterways, since the VC would almost certainly retreat through these areas. The Viet Cong had succeeded in disrupting our supply lines to Bearcat, so we could only be supplied via chopper. Ammo, C-rations, and occasionally a few cases of beer were the only items brought in. The beer was essential because the water had to be trucked in and the roads became impassable. Because many of the bridges were blown, we relied on CDS, Chinook Delivery Service.

Luckily we had more than enough AV-gas as we had just had our gas bladders filled a few days before. We would be able to operate for about a week and a half without being resupplied with gas. Because our airboats had airplane engines, our gas was JP-4, aviation fuel. Each night during the week long Tet holiday we set up ambush positions in and around the area waiting for the enemy. One night we set up a position near a main stream that was fairly well traveled during the day. We hoped we would get some action, although everywhere around was quiet.

It was the calm before the storm. A few days later, about 1 a.m., sitting quietly in our ambush position, we heard firing from one of our boats. They had contact with three sampans. These boats were moving very quietly along the canal's opposite side; the boats had three people in them except the one in the middle, it had four. Our first boat, with Wade Nail in command, let the sampans past and when they had done so, immediately opened up on them. Other boats then joined in and also fired. When we attacked, the VC immediately dove into the water as their sampans were being raked with our machine guns and M-16's, the concussion grenades were thrown into the water to prevent the enemy from swimming away. These would explode underwater thus knocking the air out of everything within a seven-foot area. We called in flares to illuminate the area and five bodies floated to the surface. One was a young girl about 15 or 16 years old. We fished her and the rest of the bodies out. We brought everything back to our compound for a closer examination. One of the bodies was an older man who had been wounded in some prior engagement and was heavily bandaged. Some documents, weapons, medical supplies, personal letters, and a case of cognac completely undamaged, were found. We turned over all these items to intelligence, except the cognac. We later learned from the information we obtained that the wounded VC was a three star NVA General, who was wounded in a battle and was being transported to a safer place for recovery. The girl was probably a nurse sent along with him. Whether she was a nurse or not, she was holding a big ass M-1 between her legs in the canoe and certainly would not have hesitated to use it on us if given the chance. As for the "Three Star General", we were happy that we contributed to his death because it meant a few less U.S. soldiers would die in future battles that he would never plan.

After this action, we were all excited, and the adrenaline kept pumping in all of us. We had completed the mission and this time we actually saw the results. From then on we couldn't wait to get back out the next night. This would not be, however, because the Viet Cong holdouts were creating havoc all over and especially in the Chinese section of Saigon called Cholon. Help was needed to secure this area. We had to leave the boats and were driven to Cholon.

VIGNETTE 9: CHOLON

**"HIGHTY TIGHTY CHRIST ALMIGHTY WHO
IN THE HELL ARE WE?
RAM BAM GOD DAMN WE ARE THE INFANTRY"!**

This section of Saigon was completely devastated and looked like a WWII city that had been bombed to kingdom come. The attacks by the VC had been over a few days, but there was sporadic sniper fire so one had to be careful. Our assignment was to guard the area on the outskirts of Cholon with a few other infantry units until everything had regained some semblance of order. We appropriated a building that still had a roof for our quarters. The walls had many bullet holes showing the intensity of battle days before. We stayed here only two days when we were ordered back to Bearcat. This was short lived because a communications unit north of Saigon needed help and we were lucky enough to be in the area. This unit was stationed on top of a mountain and it seemed the only way up was by helicopter. This was the AO of the 25th "Electric Strawberry" Division. We wondered why we were trained on the airboats if we were continually going to be used as infantry units. Thankfully on the way there, we were told we weren't needed so back to Bearcat we went. We all made a beeline for the showers, as it had been almost a month since our last. No sooner had we finished than we were ordered back to Long Thanh and the Thais and our boats.

DATE: 2/4/1968
TIME: 1500 HRS
LOCATION: THAI BASE CAMP AT LONG THANH,
SOUTHEAST OF SAIGON

"OUR 15 MINUTES OF FAME"

Over the next few months we further cemented our relationships with the Thais and developed even more respect for them. We all started wearing Buddha's around our necks; all the Thai soldiers wore them around their necks. Some of the soldiers had hundreds and they gave some of them to us. The Thais suffered minimal casualties in the earlier action. The Buddha's seemed to protect them from harm, so when in the land of Buddha, do as the Buddhists do. Every day thereafter we always wore our Buddha's.

Working with the Thais, we were celebrities of sort, at least to everyone but America. About two weeks after our successful ambush, an Australian film crew visited us. I learned later they were from BBC. I think they were doing a piece on the allies of America in Vietnam. We all had to show our capabilities for them. The concentration was on the Thai regiment with whom we worked.

Thirty-five years later I obtained the tape from Norman Stone, our LT at the time. It was amazing to see me at 22 years old as opposed to now, a hundred pounds heavier and a hell of a lot slower.

Many celebrities visited the Thais, and by association we began getting handshakes too. The Executive Officer of the Thai unit was Naron Kittakachorn the son of Thonat Kittakachorn, who was the Prime Minister of Thailand. On a visit to his son's unit he gave an award to the American Advisor, Thomas O'Connor, for his help and bravery in the successful battle that occurred earlier. The award was the Order of the Elephant, Thailand's highest medal, awarded only by the king, His Majesty Bhumibol. The Prime Minister also greeted us and gave each member of our platoon a small Buddha that is still on my chain today. Another memorable celebrity was General Bruce Clark brother of Mark of WWII fame. He came with an entourage of congressman. We also were visited by General Doleman who was CIC Pacific, General Julian J. Ewell, the 9th Division Commander, and his number two, Gen. Roseborough. Our fame was fleeting and through the ensuing years very little if anything was mentioned in the annals of the 9th Inf. Div or for that matter in the Vietnam War about our Airboats.

VIGNETTE 10: SAIGON

"THE PEARL OF THE ORIENT"?

The capital city of South Vietnam was Saigon. The very name conjures up mystery and intrigue. I have to say that it is indeed a mysterious and strange and at the same time a brutal unforgiving place. The people who live here cover the entire spectrum of economics, from the very rich to the desperately poor.

When I landed at Ton Son Nhut in September, the city was synonymous with the country of Vietnam. At the time we didn't even see the sights as we traveled through it to the 90th Replacement Battalion at Long Binh.

When we became a viable unit, we traveled through the city many times going from place to place. We were sent east of the city, west of the city, north and south all too various locations that needed us. Because the airboats operated in the Rung Sat Special Zone, our location allowed some of us to go into the city, although rarely. When we were stationed under the bridge, we had more chances to go.

I remember that when we left Tan Tru because our boats finally arrived from the States, we went through every part of the city. We drove by the famous Continental Hotel and saw many wealthy customers, dressed in white suits, military officers immaculate in their uniforms, beautifully groomed European women but strangely no Vietnamese, other than waiters. It was surreal to see this and then us, a slovenly bunch, going by in a two and a half ton truck. Driving down Tu Do Street was another experience. There were mucho bars, a multitude of stores, stands, and hookers EVERYWHERE!! We weren't allowed any free samples. We continued on and "lo and behold" we came to a TRAFFIC LIGHT. This was momentous for it was the first traffic light we had seen in many moons. We all took pictures of it. Proceeding on, we entered very exclusive section of Saigon. The houses were all large and very beautiful, they were all behind high walls and every house was gated. I think that the wealthy citizens and the diplomatic community lived here. I wonder what these houses looked like after TET. Knowing the gooks, they probably were bribed by the wealthy homeowners to leave this area alone.

The next time we went to Saigon, a few days after the TET, we were sent to Cholon, the Chinese section of Saigon. In reality Saigon was two cities divided by the Saigon River. Ninety five percent of all the Chinese in South Vietnam lived in the most devastated part of the city. The Viet Cong used this section as a staging area for their attacks on the rest of the city. We were assigned to guard the outer rim and lived in an abandoned, bombed, and machine-gunned building. There was sporadic contact with the enemy, but for us it was quiet. After two days we were recalled to Bearcat. I didn't get back to Saigon until our newest Lieutenant asked me to be his driver.

VIGNETTE 11: MAI LOAN HOTEL

"BEWARE THE IDES OF MARCH"

It was now the middle of March and we had just gotten a new lieutenant, Larry Kuhns from Texas. For some reason I became his driver, and one day he said, "Let's go to Saigon". He really had to go to MACV Headquarters in Long Binh, but who was I to question. After stopping off at MACV for about five minutes, off we went to Saigon. He knew a place called the Mai Loan Hotel in the center of Saigon. The LT was sure there would be no problem in getting a room, but my main function was to watch his back. Where the hell were we going!! We checked in and like the LT said, there was no problem. I met a very nice bar girl whose name was Vu Ti Hau, and she was a very pretty lady. I looked forward to a very nice evening. What I didn't know was that Larry had a slight drinking problem. That's what he meant about watching his back.

On the top floor of the Hotel was a beautiful Bar & Restaurant with magnificent view that looked out over the city. It gave us a great floorshow. We could see explosions in the distance; whether the Vietcong or our troops were the recipients we couldn't tell. We could see tracers from Puff the Magic Dragon, a C-47 with miniguns, streaming down on the enemy like a red waterfall. The Moon was also impressive looking. It was orange in color and added to the surreal light show across the city.

Many Officers and American civilian personnel, who I presume were government employees, hung out here. I was sitting at a table with LT, who was slugging down three drinks to my one and becoming more and more inebriated. There was a guy in civvies at the next table and Larry started ripping the Navy, Coast Guard, and Marines. The other guy kept nodding his head at these assertions. The LT. finally got around to the Air Force saying, "it sucks a big one too" or something like that. With those words, the man gets up on his feet, walks over, grabs the Lt. and hauls off a punch that sends the Larry into la la land. Standing over the unconscious body, the guy says, "I'm a Colonel in the Air Force and no snot-nose army lieutenant is going to say anything bad about the Air Force". I saw that Lt. Kuhns was tired of playing "the horizontal Lieutenant", so I picked him up, threw him over my shoulder, and carried him to his room. He probably dreamt of conquering the world.

Late the next morning we drove back to Bearcat with the LT wondering why his jaw was sore. I told him he must have slept on it! Upon arrival at the HQ of the Engineers I was told that the First Sergeant wanted to see me.

I reported to First Sergeant Claude T. Crowder's office. All the clerks were typing, but one told me to stand at attention, the FS would be with me shortly. I was about to tell the REMF clerk to go "FUCK HIMSELF" when Crowder called me into his office. He asked me to explain why I was AWOL? I was perplexed and replied that I had no idea what he was talking about! Last night I was supposed to be on guard duty and was nowhere to be found. I said that I had just gotten in from the field and the LT wanted me to drive him to MACV and then to Saigon where he had some important business with a Colonel. He just looked at me and asked if I had seen the duty roster? I said "no", and he said, "I certainly didn't deserve my promotion to E-5 that just came through" and ripped up the papers before my eyes. He also said I would be on shit burning detail for a week, and if I had to go into the field the job would be awaiting my return. I was then dismissed. I considered myself lucky not to have received an Article 15 or worse.

During the next few weeks, we went back and forth to Saigon a few more times. One day Lt. Kuhns got promoted to Captain and our trips to Saigon ended. This turn of events did not make me unhappy, although I did miss seeing Hau, my friendly neighborhood bargirl.

The next time I was in Saigon was when I flew home and left from Ton Son Nhut for the last time.

DATE: 2/25/68
TIME: 1100 HRS
LOCATION: THAI BASE CAMPAT LONG THANH,

BEER, BOOZE, AND SOMETIMES GRASS,
IT AIN'T PARADISE!

WATER! It was horrible to drink. For that matter it was horrible to live in too, but once in a while you needed it.

One day not too long after we got our boats, we were interrupted by one of the platoon members, which one I can't remember. He had just gotten back from a beer run to Bearcat, and had purchased an ice chest from the PX. This was a stroke of genius for we all were trying to keep our beer cool, as refrigeration was non-existent in the field. Beer and soda was the only drink of choice to keep us from dehydrating in the oppressive Vietnamese sun. We needed beer to brush our teeth. When we would wake, the first thing we would do is "pop a top", taking a swig to rinse out our mouths, then spit it out, and down the rest. We always tried to follow the proverb;" waste not want not".

Water, which had to be trucked in via a tank truck, was so heavily treated with chemicals, tasted horrible; thus the reason we drank beer and soda. By the end of the week we all had our own personal ice chests. Ice was no problem because the locals sold it. The only problem with the ice was that the water they used to make it was of a questionable nature. You were careful not to ingest any. There was an icehouse a few miles away, and the Vietnamese, always resourceful, sold it in large blocks to us. On a daily basis we would replenish the ice. This was a true luxury—a cold beer or soda on a sweltering day.

As it happened, we discovered that the coolers fit precisely between the ribs on the boats right in front of our seats. At any time, either on a mission or in camp we could enjoy a "cold one". On missions you only carried soda in your coolers. We made up for the weight by carrying a box or two less of ammo, which we hoped we didn't need.

Drinking and driving was prohibited so you kind of followed orders. We did not want to be impaired on a mission; your life as well as that of your buddies depended on this and everyone knew it.

A few words should be said about the ability to obtain beer and for that matter booze. At Bearcat and all the main base camps, we had what was known as a CLASS VI store. As an enlisted man you were entitled to buy a case or two of beer when available. Booze was restricted to Officers. At the beginning of each month this store would get a large shipment of beer. When I say large, I mean LARGE, BIG, HUGE! 20 TO 40 pallets of various beers. Each pallet held 40-50 cases of beer, and each pallet a different brand. In the first two weeks the pallets of Hamms, Bud, Schlitz, Schaefer, Rheingold, Miller, and eventually the Ballentine were gone leaving the horrible San Miguel. This was a Philippine beer and even 33 or bam e baa, the Vietnamese beer, tasted better. The most important thing was to make sure you loaded up with enough beer to carry us through till the beginning of the following month, because if you didn't, you would be drinking a lot of soda, or, worse yet, water!

One thing we never did was," piss off" the Class VI personnel. They were the most popular people in Nam.

We would cultivate their friendship and as a result they would sell us booze when no one was looking. They were an invaluable and indispensable part of the war effort. When we built our bar off the back of our hooch at Bearcat, the Class VI people drank free; we got the booze from them.

Beer and soda were the chief liquid replacement for sweat, and this was really a necessity of life, not a luxury, although if we drank too much, well . . . .

Although Beer and Booze were used recreationally, Grass was also in big demand. The best marijuana was grown in the very land where we were vacationing, and believe me when I say the best, I MEAN THE BEST! You were able to buy regular packs of American cigarettes, sans tabac, but replaced with the strongest grass one could ask for. These cigarettes even had the cellophane wrapper on them; what masters of deception the Vietnamese people were.

In our platoon we had the Beer drinkers and the Pot smokers. The majority of the platoon drank and did not smoke. Nobody cared one way or the other except with the caveat that no one would partake of anything other than soda or water just before and during a mission. We all had to rely on one another to survive and we all knew it!

This law was never broken in the time I spent there. I guess that character does count in certain situations, especially when your life is at stake.

VIGNETTE 12:
GOURMET DINING

"TWO ALL BEEF PATTIES SPECIAL SAUCE LETTUCE CHEESE . . ."

Eating regular meals was basically unknown to us. This was due to the nature of our operations, not for the lack of food.

Every once in a while we would get our hands on some specialty foods, dried or canned and frozen. The frozen items were mostly steaks or other meat and had to be consumed quickly. The steaks were obtained from the "Navy pukes" that operated PBR's on the river. They wanted to trade these steaks for captured weapons, so we did. Then there were other items liberated from their intended destination by some very resourceful supply clerks. We would have to trade more captured weapons for these items. I can also remember that during the TET offensive our supply lines were cut so we relied on C-rats for "many a moon" until we managed to negotiate with the chopper pilots to get us anything that came across their paths. One of these items was a case of frozen veal patties, two #10 cans of tomato sauce, and, believe it or not dried spaghetti. Nobody in our platoon was able to cook except, you guessed it, me. Not only could I cook, but I was raised in an Italian neighborhood so the items we procured were very familiar to me, the only problem being that nothing was fresh. It was a mortal sin to use canned tomato sauce, but I was so hungry for something that was close, I ignored this little glitch. The other problem I had was no spices such as oregano, sweet basil etc., so I was again forced to improvise. The Thais had some spices (we didn't know what they were), but we used them anyway. Well to make a long story short, everyone, including myself, was astounded. The meal of spaghetti and veal was *delizioso*. Let me say, however, that there were no Italians in my platoon. In fact there were only two guys from the Metropolitan area. Tommy Reynolds an Irishman from Brooklyn, and me, Tinker "the amedigan" from Bloomfield, NJ. Luckily for me the cuisine critics were from AL, WI, MI, LA, OK, TX, WA, AK, and CA.

It was feast or famine with us because a few days later we obtained a box of frozen chicken. Bob Leonard, the only black member of our unit said, "It sure would be nice to have some fried chicken," then everyone else chimed in. We liberated a sack of flour, again begged some seasoning from the Thais. Now we had our coating for the chicken. The only other problem was we had no oil to deep fry. Everyone was disappointed, until I realized that we had a couple of number 10 cans of butter. We could melt this down, and we would have oil. To this day that was best-fried chicken dinner I have ever eaten . . . . Maybe it was the beer!

Working with the Thai's afforded us the oppurtunity to sample their food. Sometimes the Thais would come back from patrols bringing a marsh deer they had killed. The marsh deer was very small, about the size of a cocker spaniel. If you have never eaten Thai cuisine, be prepared to be surprised. The meat was cut into strips and marinated in a very unique sauce, heavily laced with small Thai peppers. We were invited to join them at their feast and did. The food smelled delicious, and we couldn't wait to try some. All of us had been drinking and were feeling no pain by the time the food was ready. When I was offered some, I hungrily scoffed a few pieces. Suddenly I broke out in a sweat, the searing pain and fire in my throat caused my eyes to bulge out, and my arms started frantically waving. I couldn't talk, and the Thais seeing this, broke into hysterical laughter. The food was unbelievably HOT! I was searching for something to drink to put out the fire and was handed a glass of liquid, which I hurriedly quaffed down. This liquid was called makong, a Thai liquor. This immediately grabbed my attention but it did alleviate the searing pain, somewhat. Gradually my throat and vocal cords started to work again, although raspingly! What was so amazing was that the Thais were popping down the meat like candy. They were also dipping the pieces in a very hot sauce because the meat wasn't spicy enough, and was further supplemented by a few more raw Thai chilies. By the end of the feast no one felt the pain of the spicy food since between beer and Thai liquor we all were well anesthetized. Such was our intro to cuisines of the orient, and to this day I am very careful when ordering in Thai restaurants.

VIGNETTE 13:
A QUINTESSENTIAL ITEM

"I OPENED A CAN OF WORMS"

Many items were essential, but by far the most essential item, next to our weapon, was the P-38. No! This was not the WWII twin-engine fighter plane. This was a hinged metal blade, can opener. Everyone carried one on his dog tag chain. This seemingly mundane piece of metal was at times the only thing between you and nourishment. It was the key to gastronomic contentment if you considered ham and lima beans or spaghetti and meatballs or franks and beans a gourmet meal. It opened the peanut butter or jelly or cracker cans, wonderful pork, turkey, or chicken loaves, and our dessert of canned fruit cocktail, pears, peaches or apricots. This could only be accessed with one of these little insignificant tools.

Yes! C-RATIONS, those boxes that contained cans that gave you a full balanced meal. C-rations, the meals that kept on giving, the runs, agita, and also contentment. Yes, some of the platoon members actually loved them, and yes, many times we traded them to the gooks for beer, even though they would probably end up in Charlie's possession.

The P-38 is a little over an inch in length with a slot just below the blade. When folded, it is approximately ½ an inch thick. The blade is curved inward and hinged, opening to ninety degrees. With the blade open, the slot is fitted on the lip of can. Pressure is applied and the blade cuts through the metal top. You work the blade around the top of can until the top is cut free. Once removed the can reveals its reward of delight. If for some reason you lost your P-38 and had to use your bayonet your chances of injury were greatly increased, so you always made sure that your P-38 was in a secure place.

When a hot meal was desired, you would cut the top of an empty C-rat can, place a piece of C-4 (plastic explosive) in it and light it. You instantly had a little stove with a white-hot fire that burned fast and would heat up the rations to the proper temperature.

During the TET offensive of "68," we lived almost entirely on C-RATS for 2 or 3 weeks until supplies could be trucked in. Ammo, C-rats, and beer were the only items we could get because these items fit nicely on the choppers that supplied us daily.

VIGNETTE 14:
ONE OF THE FEW PLUS'S

"UNA GADA DA VIDE IT"

Along with the cases of C-RATIONS, sometimes we would be sent what was called an SP (sundry pack). We all looked forward to this for in the boxes were packs of candy bars, cartons of cigarettes, cigars. Sometimes there was writing paper and pens, combs, toothbrushes and toothpaste, even soap, which we traded with the gooks for cokes, beer or ice. The cigarettes and candy however were most important. There were enough so that all the smokers would be able to get at least one carton, maybe two. I think that they were donated to the army by civilian organizations such as the Red Cross. Rich Rumsey was the only person who smoked non-filters so he always got the Pall Malls, Lucky's and Camels. I don't think he paid for one cigarette in his whole tour.

You never knew what was inside the carton, except candy and cigs, but were always pleasantly surprised. We were only supposed to get the SP packs once every three months or so, but friends in supply sent them to us just about every month.

VIGNETTE 15:
PX, JUNGLE ROT, CLAP

"HEY BEN CASEY, MOVE OVER!"

In the platoon I became the unofficial medic. The only reason was I could cure jungle rot. All of us, at one time or another was afflicted with this malady. One day I got so pissed off that I poured a bottle of methiolate and a bottle of peroxide on my feet and then proceeded to let the sun dry them. After the intense burning and several beers, I experienced a miracle, the dreaded itching and pain ceased. Could it be that unknowingly I found a cure for this affliction? Sure enough, the next morning no itching or bleeding. A few days later there was only scars showing.

Another very essential piece of uniform was flip-flop sandals. Most of the time we were off duty and lounging around, these were worn to give our feet an extra chance to dry out and absorb the sunlight.

The second malady that plagued a few members of our Platoon was Clap, or to put in clinical terms, Gonorrhea. Unfortunately this ran rampant with U.S. troops, as there were hookers at every American installation in the country. Large or small, it didn't matter; the entrepreneurial spirit of the Vietnamese always triumphed.

When anyone developed this unpleasant affliction they would have to go to the medics at Bearcat for a shot of penicillin. It would also go on your record, especially if it occurred more than once. You became a prime candidate for an article 15, or worse a court marshal. I asked if there was anyway that I could obtain some penicillin and thus avoid going back to the medics. I had made friends with a couple of the medical personnel and asked them if it was possible to get some.

The next time I was in Bearcat, I was given a few bottles of dried penicillin, enough for a couple of injections, and some vials of sterile water. I would have to mix it before injecting it, and I was instructed how. The reason this was in powder form was because you needed no refrigeration to store it. I had been given this small amount because it was worth a lot of money on the black market. I only used it on repeat offenders who were at risk of a court marshal. I was glad that I only had to use it on very few occasions. Many months later, the top brass saw they were fighting a battle they couldn't win so they took control of the situation by establishing "medically approved" brothels; all the girls were examined daily, disguised as massage/steam baths. These were affectionately known by the troops as "Steam 'n Cream" facilities.

The PX or Post Exchange became a haven of delight to the GI's. You could get milkshakes and hamburgers here. You could sit and watch the Red Cross girls wiring money home; you could only guess as to where it all came from. We all longed to see a round-eyed girl, or for that matter, talk to one. It was a real treat to sit and watch and spend your money. When later we got permanent housing in Bearcat, we could buy stereo equipment, fans, refrigerators, and all things that required electricity. You could buy crystal, china, jewelry, even furniture. Mostly the Officers purchased these items, or Remfs, (rear echelon mother f—s), who sent them home to their wives. The prices for these items were dirt cheap; hence it was a big business. The PX's had regular army personnel in charge, but the day to day running of them was contracted out to Phillippinos, who hired many local Vietnamese.

We learned very early not to get film developed at the PX. All of us carried Kodak Instamatic cameras so we would be able to record our memorable moments. We did this with our first enemy kill. We took some very explicit pictures. We found out that the Army censored and confiscated any thing that was objectionable. From then on, all our film was sent to the big PX in the sky (home) for processing.

VIGNETTE 16:
WRECKED TRUCK

"THREE DEUCES AND A FOUR SPEED NO 389 . . ."

Our platoon managed to obtain a ¾ ton truck from the Thais, who got it from the engineers. It got to be a real pain not having a vehicle for going back and forth to Bearcat. We had to rely on the good graces of the Engineers, and believe me; they didn't know the meaning of the words. One day, one of our mechanics, Ray Maniton had an accident and rolled our truck. He ended up being evacuated. Our truck was a mess. Our chief mechanic Mike Stapp or "Stony" as we called him had some friends in Long Binh. These friends worked in the "BIGGEST JUNKYARD" in the world. All vehicles that were damaged and couldn't be repaired were sent here. The usable parts were scavenged, and the rest was broken for scrap and sold. Stony told his friends to be on the lookout for parts for a ¾-ton truck. They would let him know. Before long we had parts for our vehicle, but we would have to get them ourselves. This was no problem, and the "junkmen" allowed us the run of the yard to find what we needed. We loaded another truck with the parts needed and drove it back to camp. We kept the damaged one hidden from the Sergeant Major because if he saw it, he would take he would raise "holy hell". Eventually we got it running and to keep it, we told the engineers that the Thais really needed it. We ended up painting their unit logo on it. We got to go back and forth to Bearcat, and the camp continuously used it. When I had to clear Vietnam and go to Ton Son Nhut in Saigon, we used it. One of the last things I saw, before leaving, was Rich Rumsey getting back in the truck after saying goodbye to me the day I left Vietnam.

Cao Lanh Canal looking northwest. Note: Special Forces compound on right, our home away from home.

Special Forces Compound viewed from roadside.

Entrance to Marina from Canal

Nung Village directly across from Special Forces Compound (Photo courtesy Phil Cebula).

The Marina inside SF Compound (Photo courtesy Phil Cebula).

Top and Bottom Left: Traffic on the busy Cao Lanh Canal.
Bottom Right: Young girl selling fruit to the "Nungs".

Looking down canal toward town of Cao Lanh.

At end of canal, the Mekong River, 10/1967.

"Up the Mekong" to Don Phouc in the Plain of Reeds.

Bob Leonard and Wade Nail handling boat on the Mekong, 10/1967.

At Tan Tru in 1967, available space for building was nonexistent so the engineers improvised and "Hooches" were built in Rice Paddies. Note the progression. (Photos courtesy of Phil Cebula)

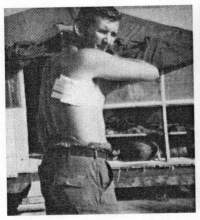

This is all you have to do to get a "Purple Heart". Holding up the shirt I was wearing.

Tail fins of expended enemy mortar round found near the spot where I was wounded. Both photos take 11, 1976.

Our trip back to Camp Bearcat to pick up our boats.
We drove through the wealthy section of Saigon.
The homes are of the wealthy and diplomatic corps.
11/ 1967

"Stuck in a Traffic Jam".   This is probably the only
traffic light in Vietnam, and
we caught it! 11/1967

Thami (Tommy) taken at Tan Tru in November 1967.

Kids at An Nhut Tan, November 1967.

Kids at Thai base camp at Long Thanh. Taken 2/1968.

Kids at Dong Nai River Bridge. Taken 5/ 1968

Launching site for our boats outside of Thai Base Camp at Long Thanh. Both from ground level and from the air. (Courtesy of Norm Stone).

Some of the dead VC after their attack on the Thais.
12/18/1976

The "Infamous" Tree Crusher which the 2nd airboat
was guarding after it became hopelessly mired in the
mud of the Rung Sat. Note that when tide came in
the crushing wheels were covered with water to 8"
from top. (Photo of Tree Crusher courtesy of Norm
Stone)

Myriad of captured weapons taken after the
disastrous attack on the Thai base camp by the Viet
Cong. The attack occurred on 12/18/1967 while we
were guarding the Tree Crusher.

Bob Hope leaving Bearcat at conclusion of Christmas Show.

Bob's helicopter leaving.

Bob Hope and Raquel Welch.   Barbara McNair and a few fans!

Packed audience.   Miss World the former Miss
Peru.

Sand bag assembly line taken at Thai Base Camp at Long Thanh early January 1968.

Interior shell on the bunker in which we would live. Photo taken in January 1968.

Our bunker in various stages of construction. Taken in January 1968 by Norm Stone.

Completed bunker at Long Thanh, February 1968.

Interior of the bunker. Left to right: John (BZ) Bzibziak, Tom Reynolds, Bob Leonard, Merle Wagner, and our crane operator.

Transporting the airboats to appropriate venues required the use of 5 ton trucks and a crane. Photo taken 2/1968

"Oh what a tangled web we weave". Mangroves at low tide. Note how dense and intertwined they are. Taken in 1968

Tending bar at Norman Stone's promotion party. Jim Wollner and Rich Rumsey flanked by two Thai soldiers. Photo taken at Thai Base Camp at Long Thanh 3/ 1968.

Soon to be Captains, Stone and Watanna. Photo courtesy Norm Stone.

Patrolling on the edge of the "Zone".

The "Rung Sat from the air. (Photos taken by Norm Stone).

One of the many streams in the "Rung Sat".

Stopping to check out a small village. John "BZ" Bzibziak looking on.

Sargent Carver, taken shortly before his death. 4/1968

Sargent Carver's boat taken after retrieval on 4/12/ 1968. Note hole caused by enemy RPG next to machine gun mount.

Gourmet cooking in the field over an open flame.
Top: Spaghetti and meat sauce.

Preparing chicken for deep frying.

"Catching ZZZ's" before a night mission. 6/1968

Dock under Bride at Dong Nai River 1968.

"King Jerry" Myhand of Baton Rouge LA. 1968

Craig Valiket holding up our unit sign at the front of our "Hooch" at Bearcat. 6/1968

Building the "Bar and No Grill" onto the back of our Hooch at Bearcat. Note: Bob Leonard at left and Paul Rodrigue sitting at far right. (Photo courtesy of Rich Rumsey).

Enjoying the "fruits of labor" Seated: Jim Wollner,
Middle: Harry Walton, Right: Jim Hurley.

Phil Cebula and Tommy Reynolds on right tending
two members of the Engineers. Note: "Hong Kong"
suit.

Airboats moving down the river to their new home at Dong Tam. Taken from chopper by Norm Stone 8/1968.

"Awaiting further orders". Dong Tam 8/1968 (Photo by Norm Stone)

Dan Lennon and Cliff Sheldon of Left. Photo taken at Tan Tru in November of 1967.

Jim Wollner and Jerry Myhand on right. Taken at Bearcat at 5/1968

From left to right: Jerry Myhand, Dan Lennon, Cliff Sheldon, Jim Wollner. Taken 4/9/2003 at Airboat Reunion in Washington DC.

"At the Wall" April 10, 2003. Thirty-five years to the day Harry Carver was killed (4/10/1968).

"Framed t-shirt" signed by his "Brothers" at our reunion. Placed at the panel on which Harry's name is engraved. 4/10/2003.

"The Platoon" Left to right: Merle Wagner, George "Red" Field, John "BZ" Bzibziak, Wade Nail, Rich Rumsey, Dan Lennon on helmet, Tommy Reynolds, Jim Wollner, Harry Carver, Mark Kizzire, Craig Valiket. Not pictured, Harry Walton, Paul Rodrigue, and Bob Leonard. (Photo courtesy Craig Valiket).

"The Platoon" taken at "Reunion Dinner", April 10, 2003. Standing Left to Right: Jim Wollner, Craig Valiket, Cliff Sheldon, John Bzibziak, Jeremiah Myhand. Sitting Left to Right: Phil Cebula, Norman Stone, Mrs. Fran Carver, Richard Rumsey, Dan Lennon.

VIGNETTE 17:
A DOG NAMED CLAYMORE

"SEE SPOT RUN . . ."

Another event was the addition of a canine to our unit. In the village up the road from our camp platoon members were getting ice for our coolers. Upon returning Dan Lennon had a little black doggie that in my opinion looked like a rat. Dan had probably saved him from being the main course at a Vietnamese luau. Dan named the beast Claymore, and he quickly became the platoon's mascot. The dog became a pain in the ass because he would get into everything, and he had fleas.

We only had Claymore for a short time however. One day Dan noticed that the dog was walking funny and seemed to fall down a lot. There was a Vet in Bearcat so Dan brought Claymore. The dog was diagnosed with Distemper and had to be put down. The Doc suggested that we take him out back and shoot him. They did not want to waste the medication as it was hard to get. A bullet was cheaper and less expensive. Dan was furious and really started a riot. "How could you expect me to kill the animal; it wasn't even a gook"! The Vet gave in and Claymore was put to sleep. All of us were upset but it was Dan's dog and it bothered him the most. He never found another rat dog, or maybe didn't want to. Some of us kept other pets, Harry Walton had a monkey named "Spider", and another dog, but for the most part we didn't keep pets, as we were always moving.

DATE: 3/19/1968
TIME: 0600 HRS.
LOCATION: CAMP BEARCAT, LONG BINH, NORTH
AND EAST OF SAIGON

FECAL IMMOLATION AND
THE PORCELAIN CONVENIENCE!

I woke up thinking that today was "my lucky day", think again. There are some details everyone had to do and today I got the "brass ring". There are certain things that one never forgets in war: your first combat action, where and when you were wounded, and burning shit!

In the Army there was a procedure for everything and burning shit was no exception.

One of the first details you were assigned was shit burning. As a newly arrived soldier, an FNG, you were given this job to welcome you to Vietnam. You had to become experts at something so why not this?

All latrines in the base camps were built on a concrete slab and were either three or four holes. In the back of the latrine was a hinged door that lifted up to reveal 55 gal drums cut in half. These of course where strategically placed under each hole where one sat to contemplate the "nature of the universe". Long metal hooks, similar to fireplace pokers, were used to pull out these drums filled with, for lack of a more refined word, shit. Once you pulled out these full drums, you replaced them with the empty ones from prior burnings. There was only a little ash left, and for all intent the drums were empty. The only problem was that if the latrines were used before the transfer well . . . this happened only rarely.

The next step required the preciseness of a chemist. Exactly one half of a gas can of diesel fuel was poured into the noxious drum. The next step was also critical; you had to make sure that the diesel fuel and feces were mixed to the proper consistency. To do this, you had large paddles, similar to oars, to stir the brew. Once properly stirred and thoroughly mixed, you applied a combustible agent; a match would suffice, and then stand back. The flame and plume of black smoke told you that you had successfully completed another mission. The smell was also another way to tell you "well done"; this smell lingered in you nostrils all week just to remind you of all you had done that day for the war effort. I suppose I shouldn't complain as this was only the 3rd time I pulled this duty.

In a related story, I remember it was mid-March, and Norm Stone or Larry Kuhns, I can't remember, had to go to MACV headquarters in Long Binh. I drove him there, and accompanied him into the building. It was another world, or at least one, which only existed in dreams. The offices were a beehive of activity, and it was amazingly cool inside! Air-conditioned rooms in which people worked, unbelievable! I was in the twilight zone! I was so overwhelmed I had to go to the latrine. I asked one of the REMF PFC's where the nearest latrine was, and he said "right down the hall", the door marked MEN. I pushed open the door, and an apparition appeared of a "TOILET BOWL". It was so beautiful I didn't want to piss in it! I had to go so bad I did anyway. When I finished, I noticed a handle on the toilet; I pressed it and the bowl emptied only to refill seconds later! This was the first flush toilet I had seen in seven months. I was so fascinated with it I kept flushing and flushing until some officer stopped me. The look on his face was one of incredulity, and if he was a Shrink I would probably be committed. Working in the rear had its bennies! "Oh to be a REMF, what lives they must live".

Thirty years later I was sitting in the movie theatre with my wife watching the opening scenes of "Platoon" and they were burning shit. The smell immediately filled my nose just as if it was yesterday. Like I said earlier, some things you never forget, an indelible psychological imprint? I also wonder what the EPA today would think of all that air pollution and was the quality standards of the air we breathed acceptable to pursuing our jobs? Perhaps this could have been a reason to stop the war on health grounds. Hindsight is 20/20. By the way if one ever questions that, Post Traumatic Stress Syndrome, is a valid ailment? Based upon my olfactory reaction in the movie theater, my answer is ABSOLUTELY; of that there can be no doubt!

VIGNETTE 18:
REVOLVING LOOIES

"THEY WERE JUST PASSING THROUGH"

The one recurrent theme in our Airboat platoon was that we kept changing officers. We had four lieutenants in a short period of time. For some reason they kept "moving on"; maybe they didn't like us or after gaining some experience wanted less action or more glory or maybe they wanted a staff job that had a men's room with flush toilets!

The first one seemed to be a figment of our imagination; we never saw what he looked like or new his name. He was there, then just disappeared.

The next one was a man named Hoskins. He was a West Point graduate and proud of it. He was a pretty good guy once we broke him in, but again after a short time he left, albeit not far. When the 1st Airboat Platoon was operational he transferred to it. He was promoted to Captain and was later killed at a line company disarming a mine.

The next officer was Lt. Norman Stone. Lt. Stone was from Pittsburgh PA, and was not an academy graduate. He had pretty good relations with the Thais and seemed a natural fit for our platoon. Lt. Stone would always go on missions with us and did not bust our chops on "SPIT AND POLISH" bullshit, except on special occasions when Brass was around.

Lt. Stone stayed with us for several months until he was promoted to Captain. For this occasion we had a party at the base camp. A Thai officer, Lt. Watanna was also promoted at the same time so we had a joint party. Watanna was an expert marksman with a .45 automatic. He was so good that he would shoot cigarettes out your mouth if you were crazy enough to let him. Rumsey and Kizzire come to mind. Rumsey and I volunteered to tend bar, you couldn't let officers have all the fun.

When there is a promotion of an officer in the Army the recipient has to leave and go to another unit. We were all sorry to see him go. Captain Stone was not going very far though, as he was assigned as a liaison officer to the Thais. We would soon be getting another new lieutenant.

Larry Kuhns was assigned to us at the end of March or the beginning of April. Lt. Kuhns was from Childress TX. He seemed to be an all right guy, though as I would later learn, grog was his problem. The only time he would drink though was when he went to Saigon, and many times I was his driver.

When Harry Carver was killed, my boat along with Dan Lennon was the first to arrive on the scene. Lt, Kuhn's had trouble starting his boat and followed us seconds later. While we were providing covering fire on the VC ambush positions, Kuhn's with Harry Walton at the controls picked up the survivors. Harry Walton and Lt. Kuhns got Bronze Stars for their rescue action, and I got an ACM with"V" device. Kuhns made Captain not long after that but stayed with us for another couple of weeks. I believe he went on R&R to Hawaii to be with his wife. When he left us I think that his tour was up and he was going into Law Enforcement.

After Kuhns we had a series of Engineer Lieutenants and these guys would regularly come and go. Any officers we had after were hard to remember because we rarely saw them, and frankly didn't care. We basically operated on our own, doing recon missions, a few ambushes, and providing security and helping the MP's interdicting sampans at the bridge.

DATE: 4/10/1968
TIME: 1530 HRS
LOCATION: RUNG SAT, SOUTHEAST OF SAIGON

TRAGEDY!

It was now April and the 2nd Airboat had been successfully operating for 4 months. We had been lucky, because the VC could not shoot and hit us unless we were stopped, and we very rarely stopped. Some genius at headquarters, probably an officer in the engineers, was going to change everything.

The mangroves were so dense the only way to get through them was by boat. Because we knew the rivers and channels, we were deployed around this suspected VC stronghold. The Thais would be inserted by helicopter and sweep the area, and hopefully drove any VC toward our position. If they were successful, we would have them in crossfire and kill many. What we didn't know was that the enemy had already set an ambush for us. No VC materialized from the sweep, and the Thais were loaded onto our boats for the trip back to camp. This was a big mistake!!! Charley then attacked us from his ambush positions to the rear of Sgt. Carver's boat. His boat had just finished picking up Thai troops and was immediately under a withering fire. The boat being overloaded with an Army Colonel, a Thai Major, and a couple of Thai soldiers could move no faster than 5-MPH, making them sitting ducks. It was impossible to see the initial action but we heard it and saw smoke. There were screaming commands over the radio and all of us were trying to move as fast as possible to help. Two other boats were bogged down with their own troops. The very reason we were so successful was severely compromised because some planning officer "FUCKED UP"!! Dan and I arrived at the scene only to see Sgt. Carver's boat overturned and soldiers in the water. There was massive confusion; the VC had scored a touchdown. I headed our boat directly at and close to the shore where the firing was coming from. I placed the boat directly in between the gook ambush positions and our guys in the water. Harry's boat arrived within seconds and started picking up people in the water at the ambush sight. Dan and I continued to fire on the VC positions and also called in gunships. Dan was on the machine gun, and it ran out of ammo so he picked up his M-16. I screamed at him to reload the MG, because I wanted as much fire as possible on the VC positions. Thirty five years later Dan asked,"don't you remember screaming and kicking me in the butt to reload the machine gun", to this day I don't. We kept this up until the gunships arrived. When the firing ceased, we joined the other boats and assessed the damage. Sgt. Carver was missing, but everyone else was accounted for albeit not in the best condition. Two boats evacuated the wounded. I moved my boat along the bank were the initial ambush occurred. I jumped into the water and started to feel around for him. I swam and dove, frantically trying to find him or his body. The water was so muddy you couldn't see spit. After 15 or 20 minutes I was forced to give up.

In talking to the survivors on his boat, they said he suffered the initial blast of enemy machine gun fire and was killed instantly. The boat turned over when it was hit by an RPG. We later found out that the rocket had gone through the boat right next to the machine gunner, and had blown up in the water, leaving the gunner, Craig Valiket, only slightly wounded and waterlogged. The RPG had caused a whole big enough to capsize the boat throwing everyone into the water. Craig remembers seeing Carver white as a ghost, slumped in the seat motionless, as the boat capsized. Two Thais were also wounded, one with serious head wounds. We searched for hours trying to locate Carver. The tides and currents were so strong that he must have been swept away quickly. We all were devastated, especially not finding Harry Carvers body.

The Army Colonel had pearl handles on his personal weapons and lost them when the boat capsized. He was more concerned with losing them than losing people. He kept frantically diving trying to find them, to no avail, what an asshole! A few days later there was a report that a body was found downstream. We all thought that this was Harry. Twenty years later I would learn that this was not the case. His body was never recovered. The feeling of devastation and frustration returned after many years. The one thing we never wanted to do is leave a buddy. Even though we did all anyone could possibly do, we still felt we should have or could have done more! According to those who saw the boat capsize, Sgt. Carver was severely hit from a burst of a gook AK-47. He was gone, dead, gone from this earth, and to make matters worse, his Wife and two children never had a body to bury or a grave to grieve over.

All of us were frustrated, pissed, and depressed at the same time. The local villagers incurred our wrath because the ambush happened, no more than 2 or 3 klicks away from their village, which we were sure they knew something about. They all claimed ignorance, however, and said how sorry they were that this had happened. They were very sad—with crocodile tears? I wonder!

When we eventually got back to the bunker, we had to pack up Sgt. Carver's belongings to send to his wife. His Buddha's were hanging on a nail above his bunk. We all looked at each other; he forgot to put them on this morning. Fingering mine, I swore that I would never, ever be without them again.

A few weeks after his death, we were ordered out of the area. The base camp was bulldozed, and so was our bunker; it was no more. For some strange reason, we didn't care! We would now be working on the Dong Nai River, a main artery to Saigon, guarding ships and barges and searching sampans for contraband. Our base of operations would be under the Route 15 Bridge over the river leading to Long Binh and Saigon.

We would stay and operate out of here for the rest of my tour. All of us still felt like shit, but we soon got back into our old routine, although reluctantly.

In retrospect one can wonder if the Vietnam War was worth the terrible cost paid. Everyone that was involved paid something, whether it was giving one's life or some other devastating loss. Was it worth it? In my opinion a resounding YES! Putting your life on the line for your country and in doing so trying to help others maintain their right to freedom is the highest honor anyone can ever do for their fellow man. No matter what is ever said, all of us who served in Vietnam DID JUST THAT!

DATE: 4/29/1968
TIME: 1800 HRS
LOCATION: AMBUSH POSITION, RUNG SAT SPECIAL
ZONE SOUTHEAST OF SAIGON

"IF DOLPHINS ARE SO SMART
WHY ARE THEY HERE"?

All of us had become experts in night ambushes and were fairly successful against the VC. They had a lot of trouble determining where we were each night because we constantly moved until dusk and by that time the sounds of our engines came from everywhere and nowhere.

One night after we had tied up along a stream and settled down for the hoped—for action, I wanted a cigarette, but there was no way because at night a match or cigarette reflected for miles. It brought to mind a quote I once read by a Navy doctor, Thomas Dooley, also involved in Viet Nam years before it became a household word, "If you light a candle in a very dark place, it shines a long way"; truer words were never spoken even though it had nothing to do with smoking.

Downstream I heard a faint sound and alerted Dan and Songwej, a Thai soldier assigned to our boat. The sound kept coming closer and closer, WHOOSH WHOOSH! Stop. Then WHOOSH WHOOSH! Stop. Then WHOOSH WHOOSH! We couldn't see a thing, even with the Starlight scope and we were really getting nervous. The sound kept coming toward our position, WHOOSH WHOOSH! The three of us were scared shitless! I called the other boats on our PRC-25 radio. The other boats closer to us heard it also. The sound went right past us, continued upstream, and in all this time we saw nothing. Gradually the sound faded and eventually disappeared. What the hell was that? None of us had a clue. Ten minutes later the sound was again heard, albeit faintly. It was again coming our way from the opposite direction, and with each minute the WHOOSH WHOOSH! was getting louder. We again used our starlight scope and saw nothing. I finally decided to call the Artillery in to shoot some flares over our position. WHOOSH WHOOSH, what the hell was that sound? The sound had just passed us when the first star shell bathed us in its glow; we could see the river just as it is at high noon. We saw two shapes moving in tandem downstream at a leisurely clip. All of a sudden I realized it's DOLPHINS! Two of them were probably looking for food or a way back to the sea. They got caught in the incoming tide and followed its flow in and were now following its flow back out. It was amazing to think that even in the midst of a war dolphins are still plying these dangerous waters. I guess even Flipper got drafted! After that excitement the rest of the night hopefully would be a cakewalk, and, bless the Lord, it was.

VIGNETTE 19:

PERSONAL WEAPONS

"ALL POWER COMES OUT OF
THE BARREL OF A GUN"

As the success of our airboat platoon grew, we began to amass weapons. These weapons, believe it or not, were mostly American WWII weapons that we gave the Vietnamese to fight the Japanese. M-1 carbines, Thompson sub machine guns, and grease guns were the weapons we captured the most.

When we trained with the Special Forces, the boats were armed with WWII air-cooled .30 cal machine guns. The Nungs were also armed with a variety of weapons of WWII vintage as well as the up-to-date M-16's. So by necessity we became familiar with these weapons. We also captured a few Chinese AK-47's and Chicom bolt-action models, which were in high demand because we were allowed to send them back to the states. We even got hold of some Chinese claymore mines and RPG's too. When our boats came in they were mounted with M-60 machine guns on them. This was the weapon we were most familiar with, and the most effective one we used. We did try to mount a .50 cal. on the boat and found it worked if the boat was stationary. If we ever fired it when moving at normal speed, the recoil of the gun would turn the boat practically on its side and could flip it over at maximum speed. Needless to say, we abandoned its use rather quickly.

Since we were always in small streams and canals, we wanted as much firepower as possible so we all carried as many weapons as we could. On my boat I had my M-16, a MI carbine, a Thompson .45 cal sub machine gun, an M-79 grenade launcher, 2 each M-72 law's, and later I asked my father to send me a .38 pistol. He sent me a snub-nosed .38 S&W Police special, which I carried in a shoulder holster. An M-60 was mounted on the boat, and I also had 10 or 12 grenades of various types, concussion, smoke, frags, and two Willie Peters. When driving the boat, it was difficult to shoot a rifle at the same time. Also it was difficult to hold the rifle on your lap for quick access in the event of an ambush. We had all these weapons for any eventuality, and a lot of times we didn't have the luxury of reloading so we just grabbed another weapon.

My father, as I said, sent me a .38 cal. Police special because the availability of ammo. All the chopper pilots had 38's, and they would trade us ammo for captured weapons. For some reason they coveted AK-47's, and this brought a fair amount of ammo plus an occasional bottle of JACK DANIELS. The AK-47's was an outstanding weapon; it was made for guerrilla war. You could crap in it, and still it would fire. The designer was also a genius in that it fired 7.62-mm ammo, the same caliber as our machine guns. They could use our ammo but we couldn't use theirs; although we had the same caliber, their rounds were shorter and would not fit in guns. We all thought that this was pretty smart on the enemy's part, and never, I repeat never took them for granted. To do so would mean a quick trip home in a metal box.

We also traded with the Navy PBR's for steaks and one time for an automatic M-79 Grenade launcher; this also proved to be an effective weapon but because speed was our best defense, it had limited use. The steaks however were very effective, and we put them to good gastronomic use. Toward the end of May we had access to CAR-15s, which were M-16s that were shortened. They were about two ft. in length, and what was nice was that they could be carried on your lap, an improvement over the longer M-16. All in all, we became familiar with most weapons through OJT, on the job training. Working with the Special Forces helped us especially with the older captured weapons. We were fast learners, and we put them to good use; old or new we were equal opportunity users.

DATE: 5/1/68
TIME: 1300 HRS
LOCATION: UNDER DONG NAI RIVER BRIDGE,
           NORTH AND EAST OF SAIGON

"UNDER THE BRIDGEWORK,
WE'LL BE HAVING SOME FUN"

It was now early May, and we had been reassigned to the Route15 Bridge on the Dong Nai River, one of the arteries into Saigon proper. The reason we were stationed here was to allow the 5-ton trucks, (the only ones that the airboats could fit on) that carried us around to be used for more important things. There was an MP unit in the area that kept getting ambushed, and we were ordered to help them. A couple of our boats were assigned to that duty.

We would be able to cover more areas as well as provide security to the bridge. The river would also allow us access to the myriad of waterways of the Rung Sat and allow us to monitor the traffic on river approaches to Saigon. This was not bad duty; it would allow us to get into Bearcat for decent chow and best of all weekly showers.

We made friends with the local kids, as always, and proceeded to go on fairly safe missions. We stopped and searched many sampans and rarely went on night ambushes. A couple of our boats were involved with some night insertions with the Seals.

There were also a lot of day missions, mainly recon, which sometimes proved interesting. I was introduced to grapefruit of Vietnamese variety, which had a very thick skin, and was as sweet as an orange.

There were ducks, hundreds of ducks, which the Vietnamese used like we use chickens; they were everywhere. The farmers must have cursed the living shit out of us when they heard the boats coming. We loved driving thru these huge flocks and driving the ducks "*meshugana*". None of them were ever hurt, but they sure got pissed.

Water buffalo were used by the farmers to plow their paddies and fields and used as general beasts of burden. One night BZ, John Bzibziak, and I were sitting in an ambush position when we heard movement in the vegetation near the riverbank. Earlier we had found a case of mortar shells near our position. We weren't sure if they were lost from a transport barge or the Viet Cong had them stashed for a later pickup. We took no chances so I called in a gunship rake our position. We had trouble starting our boat and we were getting real nervous when finally it kicked over. We hurriedly left only to look back and see our ambush position, blasted by either artillery and by rockets and mini guns from a cobra gunship. The next day we learned that there was one pissed off gook farmer who had a very expensive and DEAD water buffalo. As we all said time and again, "SIN LOI", roughly translated, "sorry about that" in Vietnamese.

We all fell into a pattern of apathy. We were going into Bearcat two or three times a week, drinking a lot, and getting bored. One day it was decided to add a bar onto our hooch at Bearcat, since we were tired of paying for booze at other REMF bars.

About this same time there was a Chinese tailor from Hong Kong who was making the rounds to all the main base camps. He happened by our unit one day so some of us decided to have him make suits for us. All it required was that measurements be taken pick a fabric, and in two to three weeks a suit would be mailed to us either here or at home. After picking the material, nice sharkskin, and paying him $35.00, all we had to do was wait.

Back at the bridge the days seemed to run together and were uneventful. We would sit by the water with our M-16s and target shoot the branches and leaf clumps that would float by. You never knew if a Viet Cong sapper was hiding in the floating vegetation, waiting for a chance to blow a bridge. Things became pretty quiet, and the more time we had on your hands, the more we thought about the going home.

Some of us were looking forward to R&R, rest and recreation; I had pretty much decided to go to Bangkok. Working with the Thais had given me an affinity for them and I was anxious to see what their country was like.

DATE: 5/15/1968
TIME: 0930 HRS
LOCATION: A SMALL STREAM OFF THE DONG NAI
RIVER

"DUCKS AND GRAPEFRUIT TREES,
WHAT A COMBO!"

In May when we moved our operations to the Dong Nai River Bridge on highway 15, most contact with the enemy slowed. Of course, after TET the ability of the VC to continue a sustained offensive posture was severely curtailed. Most of the Viet Cong and a good portion of their infrastructure were eliminated.

The operations we conducted after TET were mainly recon. As a result we saw much of the country and people going about their daily lives.

Many canals and small streams emptied into the Dong Nai River which also formed the western boundary of the Rung Sat. One of the many tributaries or streams we followed led to a small village where the main industry was farming.

I remember that on an operation in late March or early in April we were to meet up with a company of Thai soldiers. We had tied up the boats and prepared a camp site. There was a small grove of trees that had a strange fruit hanging from them. This fruit was oddly shaped, a dark green oval, and I wondered what it was. The Thais seemed to know and were all smiles. Songwej, my favorite

Thai soldier, came over to us with a peeled orange-like fruit. We tried some and found them delicious. It was a grapefruit albeit a much different variety than we had ever tasted. It was sweet, not as sour as we were used to. These trees were arranged in a semi-circle and were about six feet high with fruit in abundance. Around the bottom of each tree was a ring about a foot in width. It looked a little darker than the other soil in the area. It was night soil: human excrement mixed with river mud, and it was the best fertilizer that was, according to the farmer. I later learned that the Vietnamese regularly collect their feces and use it as their main fertilizer in all of their crops. After my initial disgust I realized how sweet and delicious the grapefruit was. I guess this is the most basic form of recycling and a very inexpensive way to fertilize crops. It's been done this way for thousands of years, and the people are still here so they must be doing something right. Songwej also confided that this is done in Thailand, as well as the rest of Southeast Asia. On the other side of the grove were 3 or 4 hooches. In one of these hooches was a boat builder whose specialty was building small sampans. It was really interesting to see how these boats were made and to see them in various stages of production. This craftsman was probably a Viet Cong or VC sympathizer, but it was interesting to watch him work.

The farmers/craftsman also raised ducks. The ducks were used the way we use chickens. As stated earlier the farmers kept huge flocks. We playfully loved driving through these flocks and driving the birds crazy and incurring epithets from the farmers. They were probably supplying Viet Cong with eggs or roast Peking duck anyway. After spending the night there we woke up and realized that one of our boats was missing. Wagner had not secured Carver's boat tightly enough and when the tide went out, so did the boat. We found it downstream completely stripped of all its weapons as well as our maps and Carver's operations log. All our home addresses and next of kin info was now in enemy hands!

Where ever one operated the Vietnamese peasant would be working his fields, paddies or orchards and caring for his flock of ducks during the day and always be watchful at night so he could take advantage of your mistakes.

DATE: 6/1/68
TIME: 1230 HRS
LOCATION: CAMP BEARCAT

THE FIRST AIRBOAT PLATOON

We had heard that the 1st platoon was moving its operations to Nha Be. They had been stationed at Cat Lai, south of Saigon. From there they were also operating with a line unit ferrying troops and doing night ambushes in and around An Nhut Tan and the "testicles, where we were before our boats came in. They were pulling security for the 2/60th units using Boston whalers as troop carriers.

There was a lull for a short time and there were no missions for the 1st Plt. The 15th Engineers were engaged in a pacification project to rebuild a school in Cholon so some members of the first platoon were assigned to provide security for them.

In mid July half of our platoon was sent to relieve them. Our operations at the Bridge continued with our combined platoons for the next couple of weeks.

DATE: 6/2/68
TIME 1900 HRS
LOCATION: CAMP BEARCAT, NORTHEAST OF SAIGON

"A LITTLE BAR BUT CERTAINLY NO GRILL"

While we were stationed at the Dong Nai Bridge, we were going back to Camp Bearcat much more often. Many times we would stay there for a few days. Showers were available, three squares a day and cold milk, even though reconstituted. There were also a number of bars that were built by different units. We would frequent these periodically, but when it got to the point that we ran out of script (money) toward the end of the month, no one would accept credit, so our drinking was curtailed. We were sitting on our bunks commiserating when someone said, as we had discussed earlier, "Why don't we build our own bar". To make a long story short, that is what we did!

At one time or another half the Platoon was back at Bearcat. We figured that all we would need was the raw material as any expertise or labor could be recruited from Echo Company. They would be willing because they were in the same situation as we were regarding money. Rich Rumsey was in charge, and he assigned specific duties such as framing, obtaining materials, roofing, and so forth. My group was in was in charge of building the actual Bar and equipping as best we could. We scrounged a couple of 2x8x12 ft. boards, but they were very rough. We couldn't get any sandpaper for smoothing the roughness of the wood, but we were able to get a couple of wood planes. We worked on the boards for many hours for a couple of days. When we finished planning these boards they were as smooth as a baby's butt.

Once we stained and shellacked, and set into place, the bar was splinter free and a nice place to rest your elbows.

Small individual sized refrigerators were available at the PX. We purchased these along with a large fan to keep the air in the bar moving. We also scrounged up some folding chairs, card tables, and even obtained three bar stools, from where, I'm not at liberty to say. I had purchased a reel-to-reel Akai recording system to eventually take back to the States when I *DEROS'ED*. This along with a radio set to AFVN was the sound system. The final items needed were beer and booze. Off to the Class VI store for the necessary ingredients. The bar ended up a resounding success, and best yet the platoon drank free. The Vietnamese weren't the only ones who could make adversity work to their advantage and profit.

DATE: 6/27/1968
TIME: 0900 HRS
LOCATION: BANGKOK, MANY KLICKS WEST OF
SAIGON

"ARE YOU READY FOR SOME . . . R&R?"

R&R was an entitlement given to most soldiers who served in Vietnam. After three months duty we could take it at anytime. We were allowed only one trip and had to have at least $150.00 in cash. We could go to Hong Kong, Taiwan, Australia, Hawaii, Singapore and Penang. Cliff Sheldon and John Bzibziak went to Penang in Malaysia in March. I waited until I was "short" (little time left in country), before I took mine. Earlier two people at a time were allowed go but at this time I could not go with anyone else. A few people in our platoon did not even go because they didn't have the required cash. Of those who went, all picked different places to go. There was Penang, Australia, Philippines, Singapore, Hong Kong, Taiwan, and Bangkok and for the married guys there was Hawaii. I was very happy to receive my orders for R&R on 6/27/68 and would fly to Bangkok. "HOOORAY"! Any day when you are not in Vietnam was a great day, and R&R was seven of them in a row.

I took my R&R in Bangkok, Thailand. At this time only one person at a time from our unit was allowed to go on R&R, so I was the "LONE RANGER" on this one. I picked Bangkok because the Thais were always talking about their beautiful country and I wanted to see it. The Colonel who was the XO of the Thai unit was the son of Thonat Kittacachorn, the Prime Minister of Thailand. Any of us would be welcome to stay as his guest in one of the many hotels he recommended. His family probably owned them. This was great especially when your finances were limited.

At the R&R center, I was issued a new uniform and had to go to the proverbial lecture on the country's culture. We had to endure the talks on venereal disease and how to avoid it. I met a guy from headquarters unit and we decided to buddy up. He was a clerk and was going home in a month. He had been in country for two tours. This was also his third R&R. That afternoon we flew to beautiful Bangkok for a whole week of not having to worry about getting shot at or hearing gunfire of any sort. When we landed, we hailed a cab and gave the driver the name of our hotel.

Our first order of business was to get out of our uniforms and back into civilian clothes. The second order of business was to get a decent hamburger and a nice cold beer. We went into the hotel's dining room and got the required elements of the second item on our agenda. During our meal, our waiter suggested that we hire a cab driver that could show us the sights. He would be available to us exclusively for a day or the entire week if we desired. There would of course be a fee, but it would be reasonable. We thought about this and decided that this in fact would be a good idea. Naturally, it was his cousin and he would call him immediately. This turned out to be the best thing we did, as the driver was also a student at the university and spoke flawless English. We next wanted female companionship and our driver knew just the place. Off we went to the Washington Bar, one of the most famous and best in Bangkok. It was patronized mostly by GI's also on R&R but was nice and clean. What made this bar so popular is that you sat at your table and were provided with a flashlight. All of the girls danced together up on a raised dance floor. If you saw one that appealed to you, you simply shined the light on her and she would come over to your table. These girls were available for either the night or the week. In effect you could have a different girl each night if you wanted.

I caught sight of a beautiful "Suzie Wong" type and immediately wanted to meet her. I shined my light on her, and over to the table she came. About the same time I saw her, my buddy also saw another girl, the one she was dancing with so she followed her friend. After introductions we sat and talked. I was surprised that they spoke English so well. We talked well into the evening, ending with the discussion of fees. Both of us decided to hire them for the week, as it was not only less expensive but also safer.

The bargirls had to go for weekly inspections to a health clinic and have their card stamped that they were free of disease. Because this was an R&R city and Thailand one of our allies, the government strictly regulated prostitution.

When we left the bar our driver started to talk to the girls in Thai. I asked him to talk English only to the girls in our presence, as this would insure that what was said was understood by all. I also said this to the girls and if there was a problem we could go back to the bar. Working with the Thais, you pick up a few words but not enough to understand all being said, so English was the language we would use. With this rule understood by all, we hoped to have a good relationship with all concerned, and we did.

The next morning we decided to do some sightseeing and we put our lives in the hands of our driver, Mr. Jack. He suggested that our first stop be at the temple of the emerald Buddha, a must for all visitors to his country.

This was part of the royal palace where King Bhomibul, and his wife Queen Silikit resided. The king is highly revered by the Thais, and the one thing that will get you thrown in jail is to show any form of disrespect to the royal family. Driving through the city is an experience. The traffic is crazy. NYC was a paradise compared to here. We arrived at the temple after much yelling by Mr. Jack, who apologized for not using English when talking to his fellow cabbies; most of them did not know English. The responses he got were interesting and I'm sure not translatable anyway, so we didn't care. We arrived at one of the entrances and all we could see were spires sticking up above the eight-foot wall.

Once inside, we were amazed at how beautiful it was. The buildings were of all shapes and sizes, there were carvings of Gods, spirits, Buddha's, and animals all over the place. The temple itself was magnificent. The outside of one building had a facing of hundreds of thousands of tiny shells. These were meticulously and expertly placed in wonderful patterns and designs on the outside walls. The doors were dark ebony, inlaid with gold leaf, absolutely exquisite. Inside the temple was very dark and high up on an altar was the emerald Buddha surrounded by lesser deities all carved in gold. I think the Buddha was carved out of Jade and not an Emerald, but I'm not sure. Another interesting part of the temple complex was an exact replica of the temple at Angkor Watt in Cambodia, once part of the Khmer Empire. This replica is made of the same stone as the original. Every way you turned there was something more interesting than the last. Our driver had a story for each statue or building or carving we asked about. We were really glad we had hired him for the week. There were a number of other temples we could go to, but Mr. Jack, our driver, suggested we go to the floating market.

Bangkok is called the "Venice of the Orient" so boats were the other main form of transportation. Everywhere

you went, you ran into a "Klong" or canal. The only way
you could get to the "floating market" was by boat so off
we went in a boat taxi. The boat ride was fantastic; the
pagodas you passed and the monasteries were
immaculate. We went through many canals that were
bordered not only by the religious temples but also
magnificent palaces and many beautiful homes. These
gave way to warehouses and houses that were more or
less teeming with people. As we turned into the next
klong, the activity was overwhelming. There were boats
of all shapes, colors, and sizes filled with fruits, vegetables,
farming equipment, radios, carved statues, and probably
anything else one wanted. The boats were lined up on
one side of the klong, and you walked on the bank on a
boardwalk. On top of a boat was a Thai policeman who
was directing traffic. If he wasn't there, you would have
complete chaos. There were also shops on the walkway
and these sold jewelry, silks, and food of all kinds. The
smells of the cooking meats and veggies were
mouthwatering, and there was no way you could pass
them without tasting something. Mr. Jack, who
accompanied us and acted as our guide, would tell us
which stores and cafes were good and fairly honest. He
probably got a cut from these vendors, but we didn't care
because it kept a lot of hawkers away from us, and we
appreciated this. He said that if we wanted to buy jewelry
to please wait until we get back to the city proper; and he
would take us to a jewelry store where we would get the
best prices. It had been a long day and we were getting
tired of walking. All of us wanted to sit down a while so we
stepped into a restaurant to get whatever smelled so good.
It was over 100 degrees and a nice cold beer would make
our day! This is where I was first introduced to Thai beer
and it was the best I ever tasted! We let the girls order
and decided that whatever it was, we would thoroughly
enjoy it. Believe it or not we did! The food was wonderful.

We basically stuffed ourselves, and when we were well sated all we wanted was to go back to the hotel and rest.

My girl friend, Lea Von Cam, was a Thai, and for a bargirl this was unique. Most of the ladies of the evening were Chinese or Indian Oriental mix. The populace as a whole looked down on this profession. Lea, or Lucky as she liked to be called, wanted to pick up a few things so we stopped at her house, which was on the way to the hotel. She invited me in to meet her mother and sister. They took very little notice of me and when they did it was a look of displeasure. I assumed that Lucky was their sole means of support, even though they hated what she did, and especially those she did it with. Being the "UGLY AMERICAN" I understood and in some way even agreed with them. After a few minutes we left and were never asked to come back. We returned to the hotel where we showered and spent the rest of the night in connubial pleasure. The next morning arising early, I knocked on Tom's bedroom door, but he was already down at breakfast. We joined him as he was having a breakfast of pancakes, when Mr. Jack came in and said that he was going to take us to a tourist park/plantation where all the crafts and customs of Thailand and its people were displayed. This theme park was located a few miles outside the city. Everyone who visited the country had to go here so after breakfast off we went.

The place was fabulous; it not only showed everything the Thai people did, but was also a school. It taught everything from silk making to Thai dancing. As long as the Park was here, Thailand would never lose its identity.

The silk industry was one of Thailand's largest exports and was started by an American named Jim Thompson. He was beloved by the Thai people and was kidnapped years before by persons unknown, never to be seen again. His legacy, however, lives on and the Thais always will remember the gift he gave them.

In the dancing school all the students are girls. Men and boys need not apply; it is exclusively for females, starting at age five. Each class is made up of about twenty-five girls, the same age. Shows are put on for the tourists, and the performances are by the whole class in that age group. Different color garments also represent the different ages. The garments worn are made of silk and the dancers wear golden crowns and jewelry. Each costume is beautiful and tells a story along with the dance. As these dancers advance in proficiency, the best will be selected for the Royal National Dance Company. This however is after years of schooling and practice. Thai dancing is a beautiful art and is exported to the rest of the world.

We then went to another part of the park where we saw how elephants were trained and the work they did. The elephant is the royal symbol of Thailand, and if one is lucky enough to see a white elephant, good luck is supposed to follow you all your life. All elephants, white ones especially, are much revered by its people. As a matter of fact, an American advisor to the Queen's Cobra regiment, Sgt. Tom O'Conner, received "The Order of the Elephant" Thailand's highest award, for heroic service during the battle at the Thai base camp. We watched as the trainers took the elephants through their paces. They showed us tricks they could do and how they were so very helpful in moving logs deep in forested areas where no vehicle could go. At the end of the show they brought out a baby. The trainer grabbed Lucky's hand and led her to the baby. All of a sudden she was riding on its back and having the time of her life. Another trainer brought out a rather large Boa constrictor and grabbed Tom's hand, and pulled him up. Tom showed that he was not afraid to put the snake around his neck, did so, and received applause and smiles from everyone there. It was getting hot and we were thirsty so we stopped in a canopied snack bar and again were served Thai beer.

Again it was so refreshing we sat for another hour and talked before we left to go back to Bangkok. We had fun and a very enjoyable day.

That evening we decided to go clubbing, and our driver knew every club that was worth going to. All I can remember of that night was the sweet smell of perfume that Lucky was wearing. The next day we wanted to see the "Bridge on the River Kwai" so off we went. Apparently Mr. Jack knew every route and tourist spot in the country. What a disappointment this was! The bridge was a metal railroad bridge and very disappointing. The trip up lasted a couple of hours, and we sure were unhappy that this was all there was. The one saving grace was that we could say WE WERE AT THE BRIDGE ON THE RIVER KWAI!!! Some consolation; anyway back to Bangkok.

Our R&R flew by and was soon coming to an end. Our fairy tale life was disappearing with the realization that we would soon be back in the land of the "quick and the dead".

We wanted to do something for the girls so we decided to take them shopping. I wanted to buy Lucky something she would always remember me by. We had gone to a lot of stores, and in each one the proprietors brought out a tray of beer. What a glorious way to shop. After so many beers you didn't care what you bought, maybe there was a "method to their madness". Anyway I spotted a beautiful black star sapphire necklace. Star sapphires were the famous Gem found in Thailand and Burma and came in all shapes, colors and sizes. I asked Lucky pick it out and told her it was for my girlfriend back in the states. I also bought some bracelets, earrings, and a nice broach for my mother. Lucky was more than happy to help me. It was really strange, I hadn't thought once about Barbara and all of a sudden I felt guilty, for about two minutes. "O' hell" we only had two days left so let's thoroughly enjoy them for no one knows what tomorrow brings" or I should say what "charley will bring".

We spent the last day taking it easy. We decided to go one last time, for a tour of the city and asked our Mr. Jack to take us. The hustle and bustle of Bangkok was really exciting and both of us always wanted to remember our time here. The one thing I'll always remember is Singha beer, and how good it was. It was a sad evening however because we both had grown attached to the girls. We also knew that as soon as we left they would be back at the Washington Bar dancing for their next crop of GI's. For some reason this did not matter. It was hard to say goodbye. Lucky and I made passionate love the night before as well as promises to each other. I knew full well that these promises were all bullshit, but it relieved some of the hurt. I gave the sapphire necklace to Lucky, and she was totally surprised, her eye's welling up. I wanted her tears to be genuine; I was really going to miss her. I asked her to put it on. To this day I will never forget her sitting up in bed with her long black hair cascading over her bare shoulders, her tear filled eyes staring into mine and one of her soft hands touching my cheek while the other held tight the jewel I had just given her. She said to me in a very quiet tone, "and please be very careful and please always wear your Buddhas". I promised her I would always wear them. We told each other that we would write every chance we got. Her address was seared into my memory, "Lea Vong Cam 262 Soy Prasersit, Bangkok, Thailand". But deep down I really knew I wouldn't. We again made passionate love and exhausted, fell asleep in each other's arms. Dawn would be coming quickly and the next afternoon I would be back in Hell.

When morning came I reluctantly put on my Khakis and was immediately brought back to reality. We had a job to do and my friends and duty called. WHAT BULLSHIT!!! I no more wanted to leave this land of enchantment than jump into a pool of boiling oil. I vowed that I would return one day. Vows, like promises, are hard to keep, and I never returned . . . . but, memories do exist, and I will never forget this magical week, especially this one night when both Lucky and I cared about nothing else but each other.

I returned to the Republic of Vietnam, it was July 3, 1968. I had a month and a couple of weeks to DEROS! I was a shortimer!

DATE: 7/4/68
TIME: 0800 HRS.
LOCATION: CAMP BEARCAT

JUST ANOTHER DAY IN RVN . . .

The 9th Division had over the last few months been building a new and larger base camp at Dong Tam. Eventually it was to be approximately 400 acres. This camp was about thirty miles southwest of the capital. It was located on the northern branch of the Mekong River, west of My Tho. This put the command and control of the 9th Infantry Division right in the middle of the action in the Delta. It was a massive undertaking and now our unit was slated to go down there to join in the festivities. When I got back from R&R half of the platoon was operating out of Cat Lai. They were assigned to check all sampans going into Saigon as well as re-supplying a firebase located in the area.

We had been getting replacements all the last few month and we integrated them into our unit. All of us original guys were getting short and became very finicky about the missions we would go on. Most of the new guys were eager to go out anyway so we let them. On the first of August most of the second platoon left Cholon and was ordered to Cat Lai to set up operations from there. A few of us stayed behind to get everything packed and prepared for moving. The one thing I didn't want to do, was go to Dong Tam.

DATE: 8/5/68
TIME: 1400 HRS.
LOCATION: DONG TAM

DO YOU BELIEVE IN COINCIDENCES?

The 2nd platoon was returning from a re-supply mission when it was hit by claymores and small arms fire. Four of our members were wounded, one seriously. Sergeant Hurley was wounded in the face and body. It looked like his lower jaw was gone. Paul Flanigan was also wounded but not seriously. Later we would see Hurley in the hospital and were amazed to see that his facial wound was not as bad as we thought.

At the same time the 1st platoon was also ambushed as they were pulling security for Boston Whalers carrying troops. There was one death and a few wounded and in the fight four members were hit. All in all it was a real bad day for both platoons. The tactics that were now employed by the boats continued to compromise the main protection we had, namely that of speed. Carrying troops and equipment and supplies were the one thing we should not do. This was why we "short timers" looked for ways to avoid those missions. No one wanted to get killed or wounded with weeks to go before leaving this paradise. God help the FNG's!

DATE: 8/15/68
TIME: 1030 HRS.
LOCATION: CAMP BEARCAT, NORTHEAST OF SAIGON

I WILL NOT LET THE DOOR HIT ME IN THE ASS!

The Headquarters of the 9th Division was moving rapidly south to Dong Tam. The Second Airboat and 1st platoon were scheduled to merge into one and combine operations out of there.

I had gotten back from Bangkok several weeks ago when the First Sergeant Claude T. Crowder summoned me to his office. I had a previous run-in with him months before about duty rosters, specifically guard duty, and pretty much avoided him after that. This was a command performance, and I had better "hustle my sorry ass" quickly to his office.

The Red Cross had made arrangements for me to get special Emergency Leave home, as my Father was going to have eye surgery the next day, and I would be needed to help my mother, who was severely disabled. I was to report to Tan Son Nhut and proceed with top priority to San Francisco, then home to Newark. The leave was for 30 days. Knowing that I was short and was going to DEROS on September 28, I asked the first sergeant, if there was any way I could clear country now instead of flying back thirty days later only to clear again. It would save the Army beaucoup bucks. The First Sergeant said it was OK with him, but he doubted that I could get all the clearances before I had to report to my plane, "BUT YOU CAN TRY". Armed with my orders, Rich Rumsey, and a jeep I headed for MACV to start clearing. I had no chance to say goodbye to everyone, as they were all over the place, and I had to leave most of my stuff including my Akai reel to reel tape recorder, clothes, a chicom bolt action rifle and other accumulated items because I didn't have time to pack.

To make a long story short, I left the country with only the clothes on my back and what I could carry in a small gym bag. I also had to surrender my "police special" as I didn't have the proper paperwork. It was a small price to pay for leaving. I said goodbye to Rich and he said he would pack and send my stuff later, and especially my Hong Kong suit that was not in yet, and say goodbye to all for me. Looking at him, I felt like a real shit for leaving everyone, but I was elated to be leaving this hell hole of a country, praying that they all would make it back, and for the most part all did.

It was amazing as soon as the Plane was out of .50 cal machine gun range, there was a HUGE collective "SIGH" of relief from everyone on the plane. We had survived Viet Nam, and I never looked back!

DATE: 8/ 16 /68
TIME: WHO CARES!
LOCATION: THE TRIP HOME

"DREAMIN I'M ALWAYS DREAMIN"

Once settled on the flight home, I started to think of the past year. The first thing that came to mind was the vast dichotomy between my flying to and flying from Viet Nam.

When I got on the plane at McGuire AFB in New Jersey, I felt that the world and all the people in it had conspired against me. There was no way I can explain the fear and terror of going off to fight a war in Vietnam. I was never as scared as I was that day. I thought that things could not have gotten any worse, and therefore things would only get better. Boy was I wrong!

The plane on which I was to travel to Vietnam was an Air Force 151 Star lifter. It was impressive and foreboding in its gray, almost black, look. The interior was fitted with rows of functional seats and not much else. I sat next to another PFC whom I had not met before. In fact there was no one on the plane that I had met before. We struck up a friendship as we were both going to the First Cav, or so our orders said.

Looking at my bleak surroundings, I realized that we were in a long tube and with no windows. We were told that we were not to get out of our seats until we reached Elmendorf AFB in Alaska. It was a mere 3 or 4 hours away so we should try and get some sleep.

Our flight plan was for us to leave McGuire AFB and to proceed to Elmendorf AFB then on to Tokota in Japan and finally to Ton Son Nhut in Saigon RVN. The weather was dank dark and drizzly all the way. It was the itinerary to hell!

We landed at Elmendorf in Alaska, and I was impressed. This was the first time I had ever seen snow capped mountains. They ringed the huge valley where we were. We stopped here to get refueled, then on to Japan. Another refueling stop, then on to Vietnam.

The flight home from the "the land of the quick and the dead" was as different as it was almost comical. First was the plane itself, a Pan Am 707 charter with real live "round eye" stewardesses. We all thought we had died and went to heaven and were attended to by beautiful angels.

Our flight plan was that we would fly directly to Honolulu HI, stay for refueling where we could also stretch our legs during our two hour layover. We would then fly to Oakland Army Air terminal outside of San Francisco CA.

It was bright and sunny and gorgeous all of the way, the omen of all omens?

DATE: 8/16 /68
TIME: 2100 HRS
LOCATION: OAKLAND/ SAN FRANCISCO, USA

"ONE O'CLOCK, TWO O'CLOCK, THREE O'CLOCK ROCK . . ."

We landed at Oakland in the dead of night! All of us were relieved and inwardly overjoyed to be landing in the States. There were times when I thought that I would never make it; I felt real, real good.

Because I had priority orders, I went to the head of the line. My processing back into life had begun. I was afraid to dream about it, in case it wasn't true.

First I was fitted with a new and proper uniform, Army dress greens, with the appropriate patches and ribbons sewn on. These people who worked for the quartermasters were very organized, and in a little over two hours I found myself in a cab on the way to San Francisco International bound for Newark, NJ and home.

At the Airport I showed my orders to the American Airlines ticket counter and they made all the arrangements. My flight however was not going to leave for two and a half hours. All I wanted to do was just to sit down, catch my breath, and relax for a while. I let the knowledge sink in that I was really back home. While taking in the strange view, I spotted another green uniform sitting nearby. His shoulder patch told me he was with the 1st Air Cavalry division. I walked over and exchanged greetings. I found out the soldier was from Long Island and was going home. To this day I can't remember his name. The only thing I can remember is how we managed NOT to end up in jail. We were sitting there talking when a real long haired hippie and his girl friend walked by. They both flashed us peace signs followed by the bird. My friend got up and grabbed the guy's shoulder, both immediately turned and gave him a shitty smile. They asked;" What the fuck do you want, baby killer"? With those ignoble words, my friend's fist smashed into the guys face! Both of the flower children simultaneously hit the floor. The scuzzball had his other hand down the back of his girlfriend's jeans and between her legs. The force of my friend's punch knocked them both to the ground like two bowling pins. The only thing I could think of was to *didi* out of there before the police came, and that is what we did! An hour later both of us went our separate ways, never to see each other again.

He probably became a wealthy Psychologist specializing in anger management.

VIGNETTE 20:
MODES OF TRANSPORT

409,409,4-SPEED POSI-TRACTION 409 . . . NOT!

In the Army you are introduced to many modes of transportation. Ground and air transportation were an essential part of getting to where you were needed.

The first day I arrived at Fort Bragg for basic training until the day I landed back at Newark, I utilized almost every mode of transport developed at the time.

I was ordered to report to the induction center in Newark, NJ. We then boarded a bus bound for Ft. Dix. Upon arrival we were told that there was no room for us so we must board another bus. I thought they were going to send us back home because they didn't need us. Boy was I wrong; we kept heading south, and south, and south. When the bus stopped, we were in North Carolina, Fort Bragg to be exact. This was where we would do our Basic Training. During the eight weeks there, the only mode of transport was our own feet. Running, marching, jumping, but never walking. If we were caught walking you became very intimate with the ground, as you had to do as many push-ups as the Drill Sergeant had hair on his head. When Basic was done we got on another Bus that was waiting for us at the assembly area. I thought we might get some leave, but instead we were again going, you guessed it, south. This time we ended up in South Carolina at Fort Jackson. Here we had our Advanced Infantry Training, learning the MOS (Military Occupational Specialty) we had been assigned. Mine was 11C10 or Heavy Weapons Infantry, the care and use of Mortars, both 82mm and 4.2 mm. After another 8 weeks here, we finally got some leave, although it was only 9 days, after which I would be going to Vietnam.

I took a cab to the Airport in Columbia, right outside of Ft. Jackson. All flights were booked to Newark, but there was one available to Atlanta; from there my chances would be better. I flew on a Southern Airways prop-driven DC-10. Needless to say, I was a little nervous about this plane, since it was very old. Compounding the problem, the stewardess announced,"Ya'all ain't got nothing to worry about", setting the tone for this short flight. Finally arriving in Atlanta, I went to a ticket booth and was again told all flights were booked until the next afternoon. The clerk told me, however, that I would be in Newark by then if I took the train. This is what I did and 10 hours later I was home.

At home I was put on a congressional hold as I was trying to get out of going to Vietnam. I was told to report to Ft. Dix after my leave was up. It was two days before the decision came down; I was to report to McGuire AFB for transport to Vietnam.

At McGuire I was assigned to an Air Force 151 Starlifter, a four-engine jet used to carry personnel and supplies. It was a very dark grey, almost black, matching my mood. The plane was a long tube with no windows, adding to my depressed condition. We flew from McGuire to Elmendorf AFB in Alaska. Here we could stretch our legs and use the head. It was also the first time I saw snowcapped mountains. It was an awesome sight. We would only stay here to get refueled, pick up more passengers and supplies, then on to Tokota AFB in Japan.

It was early morning, still dark and we got a cup of coffee and donut only. Here again we would refuel for our flight to Ton Son Nhut in Saigon, Vietnam. The morose feeling here intensified, but there was nothing I could do.

There was another bus waiting to take us to the 90th Replacement Bn. Upon arrival we were told we be assigned to our individual units. Deuce and a half's were lined up taking us, including myself. To the various units which we would be assigned. I was going to the 9th Infantry Division, at camp Bearcat.

My next mode of conveyance was an Army Caribou, designed to deliver lots of cargo to small places that have very short landing strips. The back door of the plane stayed open; I don't know if this was SOP or mechanical. Welcome to Special Forces! When we touched down at Cao Lanh, it seemed that every bolt and rivet and anything else not attached shook so violently that I thought we crashed! As luck would have it, it was raining so no one could tell the piss in our pants from rainwater. Airboats were next, and once these were mastered we flew, again via Caribou back to Bearcat. We also again went by 2 ½ ton trucks to Tan Tru where we rode on Whaleboats. We also were lucky as CH-150 Chinook helos carried the Whaleboats and us into parts unknown. A couple of weeks later we were back at Bearcat, our boats had come in! The boats wouldn't fit on Deuce and halfs so we had to have Five Ton trucks on which we fit perfectly. We were ready for WAR.

During TET, the preferred mode was the Huey UH-IB chopper because we would get in and out fast. After TET we used a ¾ ton we stole for tooling around and for important trips to Saigon. Another time I rode on a tree crusher, although it was floating on pontoons down a river, and we also checked out and searched a Sampan. Once in a while we used a jeep too, especially when clearing Vietnam for my end of tour/emergency leave.

My ride to freedom was a Pan Am 707 Charter with real live round eye stewardesses. ABSOLUTELY AMAZING!!
  Next I rode in a Cab, then jetted to Newark on a Boeing 727 with the American Airlines logo. My parents met me, and we drove home in my Dads 67 Chevy. I showered and then went out in my 1966 Volkswagen beetle that I had purchased new for $1600.00 just before I got drafted.

ALLTOGETHERNOW!!!

  BustoaBustoaSouthernAirlinesPropplanetoaTraintoa chevynomadtoanAirForceStarliftertoaBustoaDeuceanda halftoaCariboutoanAirboattoaCariboutoaChinooktoa WhaleboattoaHueytoajeeptoaHueytoaChinooktoa DeuceandahalftoanewAirboattoaFivetontoaHuey toaThreequartertontoTreeCrushertoaSampantoanair boattoadeuceandahalftoaJeeptoaPanAm707toayellow CabtoaAmericanAirlines727toaChevyimpalatoa VWBug, . . . SOME RIDE HUH!! IS THIS A RUN ON SENTENCE?

DATE: 8/17 /68
TIME: 12OO HRS
LOCATION: NEWARK AND BLOOMFIELD, NEW
JERSEY

"BACK IN THE SADDLE AGAIN,
BACK WHERE A . . . ."

I was really beat and on the flight from SF I fell asleep. We were approaching Newark; the stewardess woke me and said we were going to land in a few minutes. It was amazing that just 48 hours before I was sitting in our bar at Bearcat drinking a can of Hamms beer. In a few minutes I would be home," who'd a thunk it"!!

My Mom and my Dad, who looked like a pirate with his eye patch, met me, and there were tears everywhere. I finally realized I was home. My parents had moved since my departure so their new place was in a different part of town. All I wanted to do was shower and get out of my uniform and into civvies. I also couldn't wait to get to Sodaland, a local hangout, to see my old friends. After relaxing and talking to my folks a while, I went out. My Dad had kept my VW Bug so off I went.

Ben and Jules, the owners of Sodaland, welcomed me home. "Anything you wanted is on us. It is good to see you home". It was early and no one was around yet.

The Paddle Pizzeria was also empty. I went over to the stockade fence and was sitting there contemplating what to do next when I heard someone calling my name.

It was Gene, one of my old friends waving at me from his house just across the street. He was having a rehearsal party because he was getting married. His Mom and Dad and brothers greeted me as well. I had never met his fiancé, but she was pretty and I wished them much happiness. Most of the others there were his friends from college. Gene wanted me to come to his wedding, but I told him that I would really feel out of place! He said "don't worry you'll be sitting at Madeline's table and you'll know everyone there in two minutes". Who is Madeline? Little did I know what eventually was going to happen?

The one thing I didn't have was my beautiful, custom made, hand tailored sharkskin suit! I went to the wedding anyway, sat with Madeline at her table, and ended up taking one of the bridesmaids home. Gene and Caroline were going to Purdue for Masters Degrees and they left a few days after the wedding. I stopped at Gene's house a few weeks later to see his mom and dad, and Madeline happened to be there too. I asked her out, and the rest as they say, "Is history".

END

GLOSSARY

AK-47	Kalisknikov Automatic Rifle used by the VC
AO	Area of Operations
Ao Dai	Dress worn by Vietnamese women
APC	Armored Personnel Carrier
Arty	Artillery
AWOL	Absent without leave
Bac si	Doctor, Physician
Bam e bah	33 Tiger beer Vietnamese
Berm	Elevated area around defensive position
Bird dog	Type of plane used by FAC's similar to piper cub
C-4	Plastic explosive. Used for heating c-rats
Chieu Hoi	"open arms" BS program to welcome Vietcong defectors
Chop-Chop	Food of any kind
Chopper	Slang for helicopters
CIDG	Civilian irregular defense- Nungs,Cambodians
C-rats	C-Rations
Cyclo	A Vietnamese pedicab, similar to rickshaw Attached to a motor bike
DaiWe	Vietnamese Captain
DEROS	Date Eligible to Return from Overseas

DiDi Mau	Vietnamese-roughly translated, Get out of here!
Dinkey Dau	Crazy, Looney, Not playing with a full deck
Dustoff	Medical evacuation chopper
FAC	Forward Air Controller
FNG's	New arrivals in RVN, F—ing new guys
Frag	Fragmentation hand grenade
FSB	Fire support base
FTA	"F—k the Army" Term used to express disgust
Fubar	F—ed up Beyond All Recognition
Gook	Derogatory term for Vietnamese, mainly used to describe the enemy
Grunts	Infantryman
HE	High Explosives
Hooch	Living Quarters, huts, house etc.
Huey	UH-1 Helicopter
Jolly Green Giant	Chinook helicopter ch-47
KIA	Killed in action
Klicks	Kilometers
KP	Kitchen Police or duty
La Day	Vietnamese-roughly translated, Come here!
LAW	Light anti tank weapon an M-72
Loach	Light observation helicopter
LP	Listening post-nighttime position to listen For enemy movement
LRRP	Long range reconnaissance patrol
LZ	Landing zone
MACV	Military Assistance Command Vietnam

Mama san	Older Vietnamese woman in charge
MI	Military Intelligence-an oxymoron?
MIA	Missing in Action
MOS	Military Occupational Specialty
NCO	Non-Commissioned Officer
Numba'1	The best number,' first class
Numba' 10	The worst, lousy, bad
Nuoc Mam	Vietnamese fish sauce, similar to our Ketchup, smells disgusting
NVA	North Vietnamese Army Regulars
Papa san	Vietnamese male, head of family
Piastres	Vietnamese unit of currency
Puff the Magic Dragon	C-47 armed with mini-guns
Punji stake	Sharpened bamboo stake smeared w/excrement—an effective booby trap
R&R	Rest and Recreation
REMFs	People who worked in the rear areas, Rear Echelon Mother Fu—kers.
Round Eye	Western Woman
RPG	Russian B-40 Rocket launcher
RTO	Radio-Telephone Operator
Ruff-Puff	Vietnamese regional forces, popular forces
Rung Sat	Forest of Assassins—area east of Saigon massive mangrove swamp
Script	Military money used instead of greenbacks
SF	Special Forces
SFC	Sergeant First Class
Snafu	Situation Normal All F—ked Up!

Sin Loi	Vietnamese—roughly translated, Sorry about that!
Sitrep	Situation report
Slick	Troop carrying helicopter-a huey
TDY	Temporary Duty
TET	Vietnamese Lunar New Year
The World	USA, States, home
Tracer	Every 5th or 6th bullet in a clip or belt. Used to show where your bullets are hitting at night.
Trung Wee	Vietnamese Lieutenant
VC	Viet Cong
WAR	Water, Assault, Recon—2nd Airboat platoon patch
Willie Peter	White phosphorous grenade or Artillary shell
XO	Executive officer
Zap	To kill

ROSTER

THE 2nd AIRBOAT PLATOON INITIAL MEMBERS

Nail, Wade T.

Leonard, Robert E.*

Wagner, Merle E.

Bzibziak, John S.

Sheldon, Clifford A.

Reynolds, Thomas B.*

Bitela, Jason D.*

Lennon, Daniel F.

Cebula, Phillip J.

Wollner, James P.

Valiket, Craig D.

Carver, Harry F.

Fields, George P. *

Kizzire, Mark

Rumsey, Richard

Rodrigue, Paul *

Walton, Harry

Caughlin, Dennis*

Joined 2ND Airboat platoon after initial group of 18

Myhand, Jerry

Stapp, Michael *

Stone, Norman Lt.

Hodgkins, Lt.

Kuhns, F. Larry Lt.*

Paul Flanigan

Larry Livingston

James R. Hurley*

---

* signifies those that have not been found

CASUALTIES

The members, to the extent known, that were wounded or killed while serving with the 2nd AIRBOAT PLATOON in the Republic of Viet Nam 1967-1968.

James P. Wollner	Wounded	15 Nov. 1967
Paul Rodrigue	Wounded	15 Nov. 1967
George (Red) Fields	Wounded	Dec. 1967
Lt. Hodgkins*	KIA	Dec. 1967
Richard Rumsey	Wounded	18 Jan, 1968
Harry F. Carver	KIA	10 Apr. 1968
Craig Valiket	Wounded	10 Apr. 1968
Wade T. Nail	Wounded	N/A
Michael Stapp	Wounded	20 Aug. 1968
Lt. Stone	Wounded	N/A
Harry Walton	Wounded	N/A

Mark Kizzire	Wounded	N/A
Cliff Sheldon	Wounded	N/A
Phillip Cebula	Wounded	Aug 6, 1968
John S. Bzibziak	Wounded	Aug 6, 1968
James Hurley	Wounded	Aug 5, 1968
Paul Flanigan	Wounded	Aug 5, 1968

*   Lt. Hodgkins was killed while serving with a line company after he left the Airboats. His initial command was the 2nd Airboat Plt.

POEMS...MAYBE

WRITTEN AND COMPOSED FROM 1967 TO THE PRESENT AND BASED ON A LIFETIME OF MEMORIES, SOME GOOD AND SOME NOT SO GOOD ABOUT LIFE AND ABOUT A WAR THAT EITHER STRENGTHENED CHARACTER OR DESTROYED IT!

DUCKS

THE LAND OF THE DELTA WAS RESPLENDANT IN GREEN. PADDIES AND FRUIT TREES, ALL CALM THIS DID SEEM.

WE FOLLOWED A STREAM THROUGH THIS BOUNTIFUL GROUND, AS IT TWISTED AND TURNED AND WOUND ALL AROUND.

ALL OF A SUDDEN WE WERE IN A LARGE POND WITH HUNDREDS OF DUCKS MAKING STRANGE SOUNDS.

STANDING THERE IN A CONICAL HAT WAS A FARMER DRESSED IN THE USUAL BLACK.

HIS ARM WAS AROUND A BASKET OF HUSKS, IT WAS FEEDING TIME FOR HIS FLOCK OF DUCKS.

WE SLOWED TO WATCH THIS SCRIPTED SCENE, THE MAN WAS STARING SO NASTY MEAN.

WE CONTINUED ON FOR A KLICK OR SO, THE STREAM GOT SO SMALL THERE WAS NO PLACE TO GO.

WE TURNED AROUND AND STARTED BACK, WHEN ALL OF A SUDDEN WE HEARD A FEW SHOTS!

NO ONE WAS HIT BUT NOW WE WERE PUMPED,
WE WANTED WAS TO CATCH THIS SORRY ASS
HUMP.

BACK WE CAME TO THE POND OF DUCKS, THE
MAN WAS GONE, BUT NOT HIS BASKET OF HUSKS.

NO MATTER THE BEAUTY OF THIS ASIAN LAND,
KEEP YOUR EYES OPEN AND A WEAPON IN HAND.

THAMI (TOMMY)

THAMI WAS AN ORPHAN BOY,
WHO GAVE OUR SQUAD SO MANY JOYS.

WE GAVE HIM CANDY SOAP AND COKES,
EVEN TIMES WHEN WE WERE BROKE!

ALL OF US, WE LOVED THIS LAD AND
WHEN WE LEFT IT SEEMED SO SAD,

TO SEE HIM STANDING SO FORLORN,
THE TEARS IN HIS EYES ALREADY FORMED.

WE BOARDED THE TRUCKS AND DROVE AWAY
THERE WAS NOTHING WE COULD SAY.

STARING BACK THROUGH THE CHOKING RED DUST,
WE WOULD WIN THIS WAR FOR HIS SAKE WE MUST.

JPW 11/67

THE TRIP TO DON PHOUC

THREE WEEKS HAVE PASSED AND WE MASTERED
OUR BOATS NOW COMES THE BIGGEST TEST,
UP THE RIVER TO DON PHOUC, SOME 50 KLICKS
TO THE WEST.

DRIVING OUR BOATS ON THE MEKONG WAS
DANGEROUSLY UNAPPEALING. SEEING SHIPS GO
PAST AT EVERY TURN, GAVE ME AN AWE STRUCK
FEELING.

THIS RIVERS EXPANSE IS TRULY AMAZING AND
MAKES YOU START TO SHIVER,
WHAT GOD OR BUDDAH HAD IN MIND, IN
CREATING THIS MASSIVE RIVER.

FIFTY KLICKS GONE, WE TURNED AWAY INTO A
VERY LARGE LAKE.

A LAKE OR PLAIN OF VERDANT GREENS OF EVERY
ACCENTED HUE.
COLORS OF EMERALDS AND OF JADE, OF LAPIS
THAT'S GREENLIKE BLUE!

THE REEDS WENT ON FOR MANY A MILE, IT
SEEMED TO INFINITY.
IF I LOOKED AT THE SKY OR CLOSED MY EYES I
COULD SEE THE DIETY.

REEDS SO GREEN AND FISHING TRAPS, BLUE
HERONS DID ABOUND.
HOOCHES BUILT ON STILTS OF WOOD, CANOES
AND SAMPANS ALL AROUND.

THIS PLACE SO CALM AND BEAUTY REAL HAS A
CERTAIN SYMETRY.
THE WRATH OF WAR WILL SURELY COME WITH
SPEEDY CLARITY,
AND WE WILL FIGHT BECAUSE WERE RIGHT WITH
ALL OUR ENERGY.

DUSTOFF

DURING A HEAVY FIREFIGHT AN RTO CALLED
INTO THE NIGHT, "DUSTOFF DUSTOFF!"

MINUTES LATER THE CHOPPER CAME AND
LANDED AMID THE FIRE AND FLAME!

A FEW MINUTES MORE THEN BACK IN THE SKY,
SAVING A BOY WHO WAS ABOUT TO DIE.

THE BOY DID DIE UP THERE IN THE SKY AND THE
CHOPPER PILOT BEGAN TO CRY . . .

BECAUSE OF A BOY HE DID NOT KNOW, WHO BACK
IN THE WORLD WAS SOME GIRLS BEAU.

THIS BRAVE YOUNG PILOT HAD DONE HIS BEST,
JUST AS THE SOLDIER THEY LAID TO REST.

JPW 2/68

VERITAS

WHEN A SOLDIER DIES IN VIET NAM,
THERE SEEMS TO BE A QUIET CALM.

A CALM THAT IS SO LOUD AND CLEAR,
IT SHATTERS YOU AND ALL YOUR FEARS

YOU WEEP AND MOURN AND WONDER WHY?
A BUDDY, A PAL, A FRIEND DID DIE.

MANY ARE WOUNDED, AND SOME ARE DEAD . . . .
"THANK GOD IT'S THEM . . . NOT ME INSTEAD".

JPW 4/68

THE GRAPEFRUIT TREE

WHAT STRANGE FRUIT HANGS ON THIS TREE
IT'S GREEN AND OVOID A PUZZLE TO ME.

WHILE PONDERING WHAT THESE COULD BE,
THE THAIS RAN UP AND PLUCKED OFF THREE.

THEY SMILED AT MY BEFUDDLED LOOK,
AND PEELED THE FRUIT LIKE PRACTICED COOKS.

"TAKE SOME, EAT SOME, THEY TASTE GOOD"

"WHY NOT" SAID I, "I'LL TRY A PIECE . . ."
SURPRISINGLY IT WAS CITRUSY SWEET!

IS IT AN ORANGE? IT LOOKED SO ODD,
GREEN SKIN SO THICK, WHAT'S IN THIS POD?

WHAT IS THIS FRUIT THAT TASTES SO GOOD?

OF COURSE I LEARNED . . . STUPID ME!
IT'S A GREEN AND LEAFY . . . "GRAPEFRUIT TREE"!

JPW 1968

FIRST DAY

CHARLIE IS CUNNING SMART AND SURE,
HE SILENTLY WAITS, THEN CLOSES THE DOOR.

MEN ARE DYING, THERES LOTS OF BLOOD,
MIXING WITH THIS STINKING MUD!

SUDDENLY THE ARTILLERY WHINES,
HITTING THOSE BASTARDS FROM BEHIND.

YOU KNOW AT ONCE YOU'VE LIVED THIS DAY
AND ALL OF A SUDDEN YOU BEGIN TO PRAY.

THIS FIRST DAY YOU SAW DEATH AT HAND,
AND NOW YOU HATE THIS FILTHY LAND.

THERE IS A REASON THAT YOU ARE HERE,
BUT IN YOUR MIND IT'S NOT QUITE CLEAR.

DON'T FEEL BAD YOUNG SOLDIER BOY,
FOR IN THIS WAR WERE SIMPLE TOYS.

JPW 9/67

REMEMBERING NOVEMBER 1963

IN CLASS WE WERE LEARNING THE FACTS OF OHM'S LAW, WHEN SOMEONE WAS CRYING AT THE END OF THE HALL.

WE ALL RUSHED TO SEE AND MUCH TO OUR DREAD, "THE PRESIDENTS SHOT AND MAY BE DEAD"!

WE ALL WERE IN SHOCK, AND GREATLY DISMAYED, SOME LOOKED AROUND, SOME STARTED TO PRAY.

THE PRAYERS WENT UNANSWERED, HE WAS KILLED, OUR HOPES DISAPPEARED, OUR DREAMS UNFULFILLED.
FOR MANY A DAY OUR WHOLE COUNTRY MOURNED, ITS TIGHT WOVEN FABRIC INDELIBLY TORN.

AS THE FUNERAL CORTEGE PASSED SLOWLY ALONG, THE RIDERLESS HORSE, SANG ITS OWN SONG.

I GRIEVED FOR THE WIDOW AND CHILDREN SO YOUNG, OF THE FATHER THEY LOST TO A BLAST OF A GUN.

IT ALL SEEMED TO END IN THOSE DARKEST OF DAYS, BUT TIME PASSED ON, AND WE WENT SEPARATE WAYS.

JPW

THE DRILL SERGEANT

IN BASIC TRAINING WE MET A MAN WHO RULED
OUR LIVES WITH AN IRON HAND.

HE WOULD PUSH AND YELL AND MARCH YOU TO
DEATH, MANY A CURSE WOULD ESCAPE YOUR
BREATH.

HE WAS A MAN WHO TOLD NO LIES, AND MANY
TIMES WE WISHED WE DIED.

SIX WEEKS LATER, BASIC WAS THROUGH. HE
STOOD THERE AND SAID "WHAT A GOD AWFUL
CREW"

WE ALL RUSHED UP TO SHAKE HIS HAND, WE HAD
BECOME HIS FAVORITE FANS.

THE DAY YOU LEFT AND SAW HIS FACE, THAT WAS
SO SAD BUT SHOWED NO TRACE.

WHAT KIND OF PERSON HE MUST BE, TO MOLD
YOUNG MEN TO KEEP US FREE.

JPW

LUCKY

NIGHTLIFE IN BANGKOK ON R&R, CONSISTED OF DRINKING IN EVERY BAR.

OUR CAB DRIVER SAID THAT HE KNEW OF A PLACE THAT WAS FILLED WITH YOUNG LADIES FRIENDLY OF FACE.

THE WASHINGTON BAR WAS THE NAME OF THIS CLUB. NOWHERE AS QUIET AS YOUR LOCAL TOWN PUB.

AS YOU SAT AT YOUR TABLE AND ORDERED A DRINK, FLASHLIGHTS WERE ISSUED FOR . . . WHAT DO THINK!

THE GIRLS WERE ALL DANCING UP ON A STAGE, AWAITING A LIGHT BEAM TO OPEN THEIR CAGE.

WHILE TALKING AND DRINKING I BEGAN TO STARE AT A BEAUTIFUL LADY WITH LONG BLACK HAIR.

A THAI "SUZIE WONG" SHE LOOKED TO BE, MY LIGHT FLASHED ON, SHE CAME OVER TO ME.

SHE SAT DOWN FOR A DRINK AND STARTED TO TALK, "MY NAME IS LEEA, LUCKY FOR SHORT".

UPON HEARING HER TALK IN A MELODIOUS VOICE, I TOOK THIS ENCHANTRESS, FOR I HAD LITTLE CHOICE.

AS WE LEFT THE BAR SHE SAID TO ME THAT SHE COULD ARRANGE A WEEKLY FEE, TO BE MY GIRL EXCLUSIVLY.

DECISIONS COME QUICK WHEN FIGHTING IN WAR AND THE OFFER SHE MADE WAS HARD TO IGNORE.

SO I SAID "IN THE MORNING WE WILL TALK" KNOWING FULL WELL I'LL CRUMBLE LIKE CHALK.

THE NEXT MORNING AT BREAKFAST I SAID TO A FRIEND, "I THINK I'LL KEEP LUCKY, AT LEAST BUCK THE TREND".

MY FRIEND WAS RELEIVED FOR HE WANTED TO KEEP, HIS BROWN EYED BEAUTY, WHOSE NAME WAS SONGDEEP.

AGAINST BETTER JUDGEMENT WE KEPT OUR MATES, FOR ACCORDING TO SOME WE WERE TEMPTING THE FATES.

WE WENT TO TEMPLES, AND SAW PALACE GROUNDS, WE WENT TO MARKETS WERE FRUIT DID ABOUND.

BANGKOK ITSELF WAS AMAZINGLY CLEAN, AT EACH STOP WE MADE WAS JUST THE SAME SCENE.

WHEN SHOPPING IN STORES YOU ALWAYS WILL HEAR, "SAWAA DEE COP, HAVE SOME THAI BEER".

SO NEAT AND SO PROPER WITH ALL IN ITS PLACE, NO WONDER THE THAI'S ALL HAD GRINS ON THEIR FACE.

OUR WEEK WENT SO FAST, WE WONDERED TO WHERE? THE DAY'S SEEMED TO FLY, INTO THIN AIR.

THE TIME HAD COME TO LEAVE THIS ILLUSION, FOR THAT'S WHAT IT WAS, MY ETERNAL CONCLUSION.

BACK TO THE LAND OF THE "QUICK AND THE DEAD", TO OUR BUDDIES AND FRIENDS AND OUR UNMADE BEDS.

FOR MANY A WEEK I DREAMED OF A TIME, WHEN I VISITED A LAND THAT WAS CALM AND SUBLIME,

A LAND THAT I WILL NEVER FORGET, AND OF A BEAUTIFUL GIRL, I JUST BRIEFLY MET!

JPW 1969

THE WALL

ALL THE NAMES ETCHED ON THE WALL ARE
MARTYRS TO THIS LAND,
THEY DIED A TRAGIC DEATH SO YOUNG IN HELPING
FREEDOMS HAND.

A FEW DID THINK THAT WHAT THEY DID, WAS A
TRAGIC ERROR,
IN HELPING THOSE WHOSE LIFE WAS HARD AND
FILLED WITH BLOODY TERROR.

TO GIVE THEM HOPE AND CALM THEIR FEARS
AND LET THEM MAKE FREE CHOICES,
ALAS! THIS WAR WAS SORELY LOST, WITH
SCREECHING,SQUAWKING VOICES.

ALL THROUGH THIS TIME SOME PEOPLE SAW
FREEDOM'S FLAME STILL BURNING,
ESPECIALLY WITH THOSE WHO FOUGHT, THE
TIDE WAS SLOWLY TURNING.

WE SEE TODAY WHAT IT WILL TAKE TO KEEP OUR
FREEDOM'S LIGHT,
IT'S REALLY SOMETHING YOU CAN'T HAVE UNLESS
THERE IS A FIGHT.

THOSE MEN AND WOMEN'S NAMES APPEAR UPON
THE GRANITE BLACK,
THEY FOUGHT AND DIED FOR ALL OF US SO
NEVER TURN YOUR BACK.

YOU AND ME WHO ARE HERE TODAY SHOULD
SHED A GRATEFUL TEAR
FOR LIVING IN THIS LAND OF OURS, WITH
NOTHING MUCH TO FEAR!

JPW 1998

MOON, LOVE, RAIN

WE WERE TWO LOVERS A FEW YEARS AGO WHOSE
PASSIONATE LOVE MELTED ICE AND SNOW.

EVEN AT TIMES WHEN WE SEEMED TO FIGHT
ALL WAS FORGIVEN ON A FULL MOONS NIGHT.

ON ONE OF THESE NIGHTS A DARK CLOUD CAME
VEILING THE MOON, IT BEGAN TO RAIN

THE RAIN CAUSED A FLOOD WHICH DROVE US APART
AND SWEPT AWAY WAS OUR LOVING HEARTS

A YEAR HAD PASSED AND WE MET AGAIN
AND AT THIS TIME OUR HEARTS DID MEND.

A WEEK PASSED BY, AND OFF TO WAR, AGAIN WE
WERE APART.

BUT INSTEAD OF BREAKING, IT SLOWLY HEALED
MY SCARRED AND LONELY HEART.

FOR THAT ONE YEAR I WAS LOST IN A DREAM
BUT MORE LIKE TEN, THIS TIME DID SEEM

THE LETTERS YOU WROTE AND SENT IN THE MAIL
WERE HELP AND HOPE IN THIS TIME OF TRAVAIL.

THINKING OF YOU AND OUR DEEP LOVE,
I PRAYED TO HEAVEN AND GOD ABOVE,

THAT WHEN AND IF I DID RETURN,
YOUR LOVE FOR ME WILL BRIGHTLY BURN.

THREE MONTHS TO GO AND THE LETTERS
STOPPED, AND I WONDERED WHY?

I QUESTIONED MY FRIENDS, THEY WOULDN'T
TELL, TIME SLOWLY PASSED ME BY.

AND WHEN AT LAST TO HOME I CAME, I GLANCED
AT THE SKY ABOVE,
THE MOON WAS VEILED, DARK CLOUDS OF RAIN
TO WASH AWAY OUR LOVE.

JPW 1968

NIGHT AMBUSH

AS THE SUN SET AND IT FADED FROM BRIGHT
LONG SPINDLY SHADOWS TURNED DAY INTO
NIGHT

THE SOUNDS OF THE DARK ARE SILENT AND CALM
THE WATERS WERE SINGING THEIR OWN QUIET
PSALM

WE TALKED IN HUSHED VOICES, WE ALL WERE IN
FEAR
THAT SOUNDS WILL BE CAUGHT BY SOME ENEMY
EARS

FAR IN THE DISTANCE WE WATCHED RED RAIN
FALL
FROM PUFF'S MINI GUNS AFTER A RTO'S CALL

THE DARKNESS OF NIGHT BORE SHIVERS AND CHILL
EVER SO QUIET, THE AIR WAS SO STILL

WE TOOK TURNS TO SLEEP BUT WERE ALWAYS AWAKE
OUR SENSES WERE SHARP NOT WANTING TO SHAKE

ALL OF A SUDDEN, A SAMPAN APPEARED
WE QUIETLY READIED AS IT DREW SO NEAR

THE CLOSER IT CAME OUR ADRENALINE ROARED
TO FIRE OUR WEAPONS COULD NOT BE IGNORED

THEY PADDLED UP CLOSE, TO WITHIN TWENTY YARDS
WE FIRED, THEY FELL, LIKE A HOUSE MADE OF
CARDS

WE CALLED IN SOME FLARES TO SEE WHAT WE
CAUGHT. IN THIS BATTLE SO BREIF, WAS IT FOR
NAUGHT?

AS THE ROUNDS SHED THEIR LIGHT UPON THE
GRIM SCENE THEIR BODIES WERE FLOATING ON
WATERS SEA GREEN.

THIS NIGHT WE HAD WON AND WERE VERY GLAD
THAT NO ONE WAS HURT, BUT STILL FEELING SAD

SAD AT THE DEATHS WE HAD CAUSED THIS NIGHT,
BUT HAPPY NO FRIENDS WERE KILLED IN THIS
FIGHT.

SUCH IS THE JOB WE WERE TRAINED TO PURSUE
KILLING THE ENEMY, THAT WOULD GLADLY KILL
YOU!

JPW

THE MANGROVE SWAMP

THESE TREES SEEMED TO FLOAT ON THE WATERS SO GREEN.

THE LEAVES WERE ALL WAXY AND HAD AN ODD SHEEN.

THEIR STALKS AND THEIR BRANCHES WERE ALL INTERTWINED,

THESE PLANTS WERE SO THICK THAT IT MADE US OPINE,

A HUNDRED OF CHARLIE COULD HIDE WITHOUT FAIL.

AND SET A GOOD AMBUSH TO KICK OUR SWEET TAIL.

A FEW HOURS LONGER THEN THE TIDE DID RECEDE,

LEAVING MUD SCARS, THAT SEEMED ALL TO BLEED.

THE SOUTH CHINA SEA SEEMED TO SUCK THE SWAMP DRY,

SOON TO VOMIT IT BACK, WHEN THE MOON WAS ON HIGH.

THE WATER WAS SALTY AS IT RETURNED FROM THIS SEA.

TO SUCCOR AND NOURISH THESE OLD MANGROVE TREES.

JPW

WHERE ARE THEY NOW?

PHIL CEBULA

Phil has led an interesting life since Vietnam. He was first married in 1969 and fell into a life of drugs. He was convicted of 2nd degree manslaughter and spent 4 yrs in Prison at the Attica correctional facility. He was divorced in 1978. During his initial arrest and trial he became a born again Christian on July 19, 1975. While in Prison he studied the bible and ministered to those incarcerated with him. He obtained an early release for exemplary behavior and then studied for the Ministry.

Phil remarried on April 3, 1983 to his wife Irene. They live in Fitchburg MA. Phil and Irene have three children, A boy Dan and two daughters Jennifer and Cheryl. Phil has an older daughter, Andrea by his previous marriage. Phil and Irene are co-pastors of the Church of the Living God a Four Square Church in downtown Fitchburg. Phil says," Life is great".

DAN LENNON

Dan and his wife Phyllis live in Santee CA. Dan is a truck driver with Yellow Freight Co. Phyllis is a classroom aide in Santee. They have two sons, Michael 28 and Daniel 30.

Dan retired this year and they plan to do a lot of traveling.

When Dan left the Army he had various jobs, working as a Bellman and valet parker in a Hotel resort. Dan said the tips were great but it was too slow a pace so I started looking for something else. I was drinking at a tuna fisherman's bar and with my penchant for beer drinking I fit right in and they took me under their wings, especially because I was a veteran. I was hired on the tuna boat because a lot of money could be made, it never worked out.

I was drinking every minute and bar hopping alone one night when I saw this blond sitting with this guy. I started shooting pool with the guy and found out eventually that the girl was his sister. I finally had the courage to ask her out the next night. Phyllis and I have been married 32 years.

After meeting her I got a job with Transcom Trucking and was with them for 17 years then moved over to Yellow Freight lines for the past 14. I just retired and plan on doing some traveling.

RICH RUMSEY

Rich currently lives with his friend Hilary in Rhinebeck NY. He has a daughter from a prior marriage, and recently attended her wedding in Las Vegas. He owns his own Home contracting company and this keeps very busy.

CLIFF SHELDON

Cliff lives with his wife Cathy in Yukon OK. They have two children. Cliff has a tool repair business in Oklahoma City. Cliff's business was a block away from the Murrah Federal building that was destroyed by a truck bomb in Oklahoma City.

JOHN BZIBZIAK

John lives in Hamburg NY with his wife Judi. They have a daughter Katrina and two granddaughters, Samantha and Mikayla.

While in Vietnam, John asked Phil if he could write to his friend, Judi. John and Judi began to write each other and fell in love. Upon John's return he went to NY, met Judi and a few months later they married. John and Judi returned to Fort Benning for the remainder of John's enlistment. They then moved to John's hometown in Indiana and John hated it. They were set to move to Alaska to homestead when Judi became ill. John then decided to get a real job and started at Ford. They moved to Hamburg NY and started a family.

WADE NAIL

Wade lives in Cleveland TX with his wife Wanda Jeanne. They have three children, Stacy age 31 and twin boys Wade and George age 28. Upon his return to the world he was assigned as a drill sergeant at Fort McClelland, AL. In 1970 he went to work for SW Bell as in installer, also got married in June of 1970. In 1973 joined the Army National Guard and left after 8 months. In 1980 joined the Texas Air National Guard. He retired from Bell South in 1997 and went on active duty with the Air Force, retiring in 2000 as a Chief Master Sergeant. He spends his time with his children's pet business and Bass fishing and lifting weights and bodybuilding. Wade is also an active member of a civil war reenactment group. He was scheduled to be a part of the burial service of the sailors who were on the Hunley.

CRAIG VALIKET

Craig lives in Hahira GA with his wife Norma. Craig and Norma have two daughters, Valerie age 32 and Cindy 23. When enlistment was up he returned to Greenville MI and went to work in a Refrigerator factory. Met Norma and got married. Hated the winters and in 1974 moved to GA where there was little if any snow. Craig restores classic cars and has a "69 GTO" a "66"Lemans and a "64"Chevy Truck. Craig is employed in a retirement home in the maintenance department. He has been married 33 years.

JERRY MYHAND

Jerry lives in Baton Rouge LA with his wife Judy, who teaches at LSU . . .

Jerry is employed with the Environmental Protection Agency. He is an avid golfer and pretty good too. He is among one of the top amateurs in the country.

NORMAN STONE

Norm lives in Southington CT with his wife Marilyn. They have 5 children, Erica 28 an EMT/PARAMEDIC, Ned 25 who is currently in the Air Force in Saudi Arabia, Chet 22 a junior in college, Don 20 a freshman in college and Chris 18 who just graduated high school.

Norman currently works for the Defense Contract Audit Agency. He attended Duquesne University and worked for Dravo Corp. in Labor relations and TRW in human relations. Norm is also an Army Reservist, asst. G-3 Ops, and Bn Cmdr and Info Mgmt Officer.

HARRY WALTON

Harry lives in Brownsville TN. He is a police Sergeant with the Brownsville P.D.

Upon his return from Vietnam he did some factory work then moved into construction and finally into law enforcement. He has been a police officer for 20 years.

Harry lives with his wife Deane and has three children, Timothy 26, Lee 29, and Rebecca 30. They have three grandchildren. When not working he enjoys hunting and fishing at his vacation house on the Hatchie river.

JAMES WOLLNER

Upon His return from Vietnam he was stationed at Fort Dix, NJ. He was an assistant Drill Instructor until he was granted an early discharge in 1968 to return to school.

Jim met his future wife, Madeline the very night he returned from Nam, although he didn't know it at the time. They were married on January 25 1970.

Jim went back to school and received his BA in Pol.Sci./History from Bloomfield College. He was intending to go to law school but never made it. Jim started working in purchasing for an office supply Manufacturer. He then became director of Purchasing in a hospital. A few years later he became the Vice President of Materials Management at a large inner city hospital.

Jim was diagnosed with Multiple Sclerosis in 1980 and retired in 1986.

Jim and Madeline have a home in Bloomfield, NJ. Madeline has been a Speech Therapist for thirty-five years in the West Orange Public Schools system. She is planning to retire at the end of this year. Jim and Madeline have two children, Christian 28 and Katherine 23 who currently lives in Steamboat Springs CO.

MARK KIZZIRE

Mark lived in Grants Pass Oregon. He is currently lives a lifestyle that gives him the most freedom as possible. He pans for gold in the rivers and streams and makes enough for his needs. Mark bought a small boat and currently lives in Brookings were he fishes for salmon. Mark has 2 children.

WHEREABOUTS UNKNOWN

JASON BITELA   BOB LEONARD

THOMAS REYNOLDS   GEORGE FIELDS

PAUL RODRIGUE   DENNIS CAUGHLIN

MICHAEL STAPP   JAMES HURLEY

HEY GUYS! WHERE ARE YA?

EPILOUGUE

On April 9th 10th and 11th, 2003 a reunion of the 2nd Airboat Platoon was held in Washington DC. All but three members of the platoon have not seen or met each other in the 35 years since leaving Vietnam. The following story is the account of how this reunion was born. It also gives a brief biography of the platoon members and where life has led them so far.

It is a story of America itself. Each member has found their place in this diverse and complex society. They restore cars, participate in historical reenactments of wars long past, play golf, attend sporting events, climb mountains, go fishing and hunting, travel across the country, have family reunions, volunteer to help in their churches and communities, pan for gold, raise vegetables and most important care for and love their families and their friends.

After these many years, bringing all of us together was one of the most poignant and joyous times in my life. The only regret I have is, we didn't do it sooner.

JPW

FINDING

LOST BROTHERS

THE SEARCH FOR MEMBERS OF THE
2ND AIRBOAT PLATOON

A SHORT TRUE STORY

By

JAMES PARKER WOLLNER

A few years ago we gave our children a computer for Christmas. My son Chris had it out of the boxes and up and running before I sipped my first cup of coffee, so much for following directions. God bless the younger generation, they are fearless when it comes to technology.

"Old farts" like me were so intimidated by the darn thing that I was afraid to open up the box. A few months later and after many snide comments from my kids, I sat down in front of it and a whole new world suddenly opened up for me.

I had been diagnosed with MS in 1974 and left work in 1986. Even though I couldn't work I could do some cooking and simple household chores. One could say that I was the original Mr. Mom. I could punch a few keys on a keyboard, I hoped the right ones, and thus the computer offered me oppurtunities where none had existed before.

I decided to write down my recollections of a time in my life that had a profound effect on me, my yearlong vacation in Southeast Asia and participation in the Vietnam War.

I found a journal/diary that I started upon my arrival "in country" and ended a little over two months later. I'm sorry now that I stopped after only two months. Nevertheless, it gave me a point on which to begin my saga. This, coupled with the pictures I had taken, would yield a wealth of memories, or at least I hoped so.

Over the past thirty odd years the utter lack of any information in books, magazines, newspapers or TV news stories on the use of airboats, infuriated me. The time had come for someone to do something about it. The Royal Thai Army and especially the Queen's Cobra Regiment was never mentioned. We worked much of the time with them. It seemed that our airboats or the Thais never existed; both seemed to disappear into the mists of time. Was that year in hell a figment of my imagination?

In the course of writing, I began to wonder what happened to everyone. Since my return to the States, I only saw one member of my unit, Phil Cebula, and that was in 1972 a short time after he got married. His wife had relatives in nearby Kearny NJ, and he contacted me when he came down to visit them. After that meeting we lost contact, and I saw no one for the next 31 years.

Memories started flooding back, and as I wrote they seemed to occur haphazardly. I started to arrange these thoughts, chronologically and the fog began to clear. During this exercise I started wondering about each face in the many photos, could I find them, what are they doing and where are they living?

The first person I tried to find was Phil. I knew that he lived in Buffalo, NY, so I started there. I found nothing; it was like he never existed. I remembered another friend, Craig Valiket from Wisconsin and again no luck. Then John Bzibziak-"BZ"—and Cliff Sheldon from Hamtramck, Michigan and again another dead end, no record. I then tried Rich Rumsey who I knew lived in Rhinebeck, NY and at last had success. I also found BZ living in Hamburg, NY, and he was still friends with Phil who now lived in Fitchburg, MA. Then I looked up Dan Lennon in San Diego, California, got him too. Dan worked for Yellow Freight and has lived in San Diego since getting out of the service. Dan was so ecstatic that he and his wife Phyllis flew into Newark in late June, 2002. Madeline and I picked them up at the airport. It was difficult to describe the feelings we shared; it was like meeting a long lost brother.

The past thirty five years disappeared, vanished into thin air. It was the most emotional experience I had in my life and Dan's too. I told Dan about the others and he said let's see if we could get together. I called BZ and Phil and asked them to meet us and Rich in Rhinebeck. Phil, now a minister, had planned a trip to Haiti with his church and BZ was going to a family reunion in Indiana. Phil then told me his story, and it is remarkable.

In the early seventies he became involved with drugs and alcohol. One day a neighbor, who was also a druggie broke into Phil's house. Phil found him and shot him. The druggie/neighbor still walked out and went to his house. Phil followed and told his parents that their son was shot and should go to the hospital. The guy's parents ignored his plea, and as a result he died from severe blood loss. Phil was charged with second-degree manslaughter and sentenced to 6 to 8 years in prison, and would serve his time in Attica. Just before his trial, he was given a bible, and he started reading it. He found God and was instrumental in forming a bible study groups in prison. Because he showed extraordinary change and led an exemplary life in prison helping others, he was let out after serving four years. A friend helped him to get into divinity school. He left school to become a pastor of a Foursquare Church in Fitchburg MA. Phil and his first wife divorced following his conviction. He remarried and now both he and Irene are co-pastors. Phil has four children, three with Irene and a daughter with his first wife.

A few days after Dan arrived, we drove up to Rhinebeck to see Rich. We met at Foster's, the local pub, and the moment Rich saw me he rushed over and picked up all 280 lbs. of me. The same emotional feelings came over the three of us. It was just like yesterday, as if the past years meant nothing, but they did surely fly by. We were really so glad to see each other; it was astounding!

The three of us decided, then and there, that we should have a full-fledged reunion with everyone in the unit. Rich and Dan decided that I should organize it because I had the time and already had found a number of us. I agreed, and there our quest to find others began in earnest. Rich had the original set of orders for our training with the Special Forces. This had all our names and army serial numbers so that was good info to start. Dan had also been in contact with Jerry Myhand and thought he lived in Baton Rouge, LA. Jerry was not an original member but came over from the first platoon a couple months later. Jerry was also in contact with a replacement sergeant named Larry Livingston from the first platoon and thought he lived in Lumber City, GA. I searched and found him. Dan was also in contact with Cliff Sheldon who now lived in Yukon, OK. I found the name of a Craig Valiket but it was a phone number in GA. I called and sure enough it was him; he moved to get out of the cold winters and made Hahira, GA his home. He also told me that Harry Walton lived in Brownsville TN. Harry is a police sergeant and is also a grandfather.

I continued searching various web sights looking for anything about the airboats. One day on the 9th division web page was a note from a guy by the name of Don Nickles. This was a name that was unfamiliar to me, but the time, names and places he mentioned were not. I decided to give him a call. Don lives in Northport, WA. He mentioned that his memory was very spotty and he could only remember a few nicknames. He could definitely remember the commander of the Special Forces unit who trained us, as well as the commander of the SF unit. I looked at our set of orders that Rich had sent to me and sure enough Don's name was there. Later I was talking to Dan, he remembered that there was a guy who left our unit at Tan Tru before our boats arrived from the States. He was transferred to a Mechanized unit with the

2 / 60th based at Tan Tru. Don had a lot of problems with the VA, and his Army records showed him AWOL during the time he was training with us. When I told him that his name was on the orders, he was elated and asked me to send him a copy so he could shove it in their faces and get his records corrected, as well as showing proof to his doctors. He also told me that a Norman Stone had talked to him (but didn't know who he was) and he had a videotape of our unit. It was incredulous that it existed! Stone was our first lieutenant and I got his number from Don.

Norm lives in Southington, CT, and is only an hour away from me, amazing! I called him and bingo!! Another member found. I then asked him about the tape and how he obtained it. He told me the story. His mother was watching the News and the BBC was broadcasting a story on airboats and the Royal Thai Army. Knowing her son was in charge of the airboats, she wrote to BBC asking for a copy of the broadcast film. Videotape was not invented or used then, only film cameras, but they sent an 8mm film copy to her. Norman had it made into videotape a few years later. He said that he would make a copy and send it to me. A couple of weeks later it arrived and when I looked at it, I was blown away! There were two scenes with me in them . . . 34 years ago! Never in 34 years did I see anything on the airboats and now to see a story with me in it, it was totally "mind blowing". I in turn, made copies and sent them to all the members I had located. Everyone was ecstatic as well; we had an actual video of our exploits. Too bad it is only 3 minutes long.

We were really moving on finding people trying every means possible. There were two people we were trying to find from CA. One was Jason Bitela and the other was Mark Kizzire.

You would figure Kizzire was not a common name and it should be easy. Well there was one Kizzire in CA, and her name was Julie. It was no relation. I started looking at the surrounding states and found a M. Kizzire in AZ. I called and again no relation. A search company, US Search, popped up on my screen and said they would find anyone for a fee. They would do an Internet search for $ 20.00 each. I decided I would give it a try, and they came back with addresses for Kizzire and Bitela. Jason's address was in Los Angeles, CA, and Mark's was in Grants Pass, OR. I sent letters to the addresses and waited. Jason's came back as undeliverable, but nothing from Mark. I spoke to Dan, and he said he would call the police in Grants Pass and ask them to check out the address. They did, but we were told that he no longer lived there but did occasionally show up. Weeks later there was still no answer. Dan's wife Phyllis, suggested that we place an ad in the local paper in Grants Pass, as she had done it a few years ago when she was looking for some of her relatives. We did, and a few days later Mark called us. He told us a friend showed him our ad. He was immediately overwhelmed to see it along with our names.

Mark lived in and around Grants Pass. He lived in the woods and pans for gold in the Rouge River; he is homeless by choice. The friend of his does cleaning for a local motel and bought a newspaper one day. She was sitting in Mark's camp reading it when she came upon the ad for Mark, asked him if this was him. Mark has since moved to Harbor, OR and bought a fishing boat. He told me that the only thing that would keep him away from the reunion is death; he would be there with bells on. Another brother found.

Weeks later I called the Veterans Administration and asked if they could do anything to help me find the people with whom I served. I was transferred to an operator who said that I could send a letter and stamped envelopes with the name of the veteran on them. If they were in the system, the VA would forward them, noting that they could not give out their addresses. There were seven people I couldn't find so I sent in 7 stamped envelopes each with a separate name. I also sent one more with the name of my platoon sergeant's widow. She was the person we wanted most to attend. I must have searched all the states looking for her without success. In my letter to the VA in Newark, NJ, I included my address, phone number, fax number and e-mail address. A few days later I got a call from the VA and was told that they found only three of the seven people. Those three were George Fields, Merle Wagner, and Fran Carver. It was great news and they would forward those letters. The only thing I could do was wait and hope they would answer. The rest would be returned to me, and she suggested that I send them to St. Louis and follow the same procedure. She also gave me the address where I should send them. I did and hopefully will get a response soon.

Fran Carver, Harry's widow, had received my letter on Christmas Eve day and was totally shocked. She was not going to respond but saw my name on the return address label. She had a picture of Harry and me, and I was the only person identified in the picture. Fran is a very private person and the e-mail she sent reflected this. She also did not give the location of her residence. She thanked me for sending it but wanted to know how I found her address. I e-mailed her back and explained to her I still did not know where she was and how the VA had helped, and I also assured her that I would respectfully maintain her privacy, if she desired. A few days went by, almost a week, when I got another e-mail from her, this time warmer and more relaxed. She apologized for any misunderstanding and told me she had a number of bad experiences with so called Vietnam vets and hoped that I understood. I e-mailed her back and told her that she certainly had nothing to apologize for, and if there was anything we could do, please let us know. I then told her about the people I had contacted, and how the reunion got started, and sent her a picture of Dan, Rich, and myself taken at our mini reunion in July. We offered to fly her to Washington, DC this April for the reunion. Her next e-mail was great! She again thanked us and said we would not have to fly her to DC, but she would find a way to get there. It was nice to know that she would be coming. She also said that she lives with her daughter in Coeur D'Alene, ID. She was going to go through boxes from Harry and find pictures and things we might like to see. She had many questions and mysteries for us. I told her that we would answer all her questions and solve all her mysteries. One day I decided to actually call and speak to her, and I am glad I did! It is one thing to converse with someone via e-mail but totally different when you talk to that person. I am really looking forward to meeting her at our reunion in April.

The first week of January '03 went by quickly. I was going through my mail one day when I saw another one of the letters the VA sent out, being returned to me. It was to Merle Wagner. The letter was marked "undeliverable". My eyes went to the address and I did a double take. The address was 2065 Griffith Way, in Fresno, CA. I was speechless!! My brother-in-law lives at 4067 Griffith Way in Fresno. What an amazing coincidence! Whoever said, "it's a small world" knew what they were talking about. I had my brother-in-law do some amateur detective work. A few more days went by and I received a call from him that Merle Wagner was deceased. I later verified this by his SS#, there was no mistake. Merle was the first member, other than Harry Carver, that died. I still have not heard from Red Fields, but maybe it will come all of a sudden, I hope it will.

Three weeks before our reunion, Dan Lennon called me and said he found Paul Flanigan. Dan called two restaurants where Paul worked. He asked if someone saw Paul to have him call. After two weeks Paul called. He lives in Albany, NY.

I am still waiting to see if any of the letters I sent to St. Louis have been forwarded so it still isn't the end of this story. I'm hoping that Mike Stapp, Tommy Reynolds, Paul Rodrigue, Dennis Caughlin, Bob Leonard and George Field will surely be found. Stay tuned!

ACKNOWLEDGEMENTS

Memories, like beauty, are truly in the eye or mind of the beholder. Many were as clear and bright as the day they occurred, while others were somewhat misty and fragmented. In penning these memoirs I realized that this story could not have been written without the help of each of my airboat brethren, Dan Lennon, Rich Rumsey, Phil Cebula, John Bzibziak, Craig Valiket, Wade Nail, Harry Walton, Cliff Sheldon, Mark Kizzire, Jerry Myhand, Paul Flanigan, and especially Norman Stone. Finding out that Norm had a videotape of our unit was the highpoint of this project, and seeing me in it totally "blew me away". Norm, I also forgive your lousy driving, and so does my derriere!

Special thanks are owed to Don Nickles whose note on the 9th division website mentioned names and places that started me on the quest to find my brothers.

Thanks to Bruce Petrosine and Doug Stegall of the 1st platoon; Bruce remembered a name I'd forgotten and this brought back more memories.

A heart-felt thanks to Inez B. Jacklin for her superior knowledge of English grammar for editing this story.

My lifelong friend from kindergarten, Roberta Fitzgerald, is also to be thanked for her final proofing. "I loved all those penciled in corrections".

Lastly, I want to thank my wife Madeline, who has put up with me for thirty four years and whose meaningful criticism kept me focused on the objective. To both of my children, Christian and Katherine, who embarrassed me into using the computer to record this "ancient history", thank you and I love you.

I love you all!

JPW

Printed in the United States
23118LVS00002B/184